S0-AHW-713

GREGG SHORTHAND DICTIONARY

ABRIDGED VERSION

CHARLES E. ZOUBEK

CENTENNIAL
EDITION

Gregg Division

GLENCOE/McGRAW-HILL
A Macmillan/McGraw-Hill Company

Westerville, Ohio   Mission Hills, California   Peoria, Illinois

Cover Designer: Keithley and Associates

Library of Congress Cataloging-in-Publication Data

Gregg, John Robert, 1867-1948.
  Gregg shorthand dictionary / Charles E. Zoubek. — Abridged
version, Centennial ed.
     p.   cm.
  ISBN 0-07-073682-0
  1. Shorthand—Gregg—Dictionaries.   I. Zoubek, Charles E., date.
  II. Title.
  Z56.2.G7A3   1990
  653' .427' 03—dc20   89-13277
                                                   CIP

The manuscript for this book was processed electronically

Gregg Shorthand Dictionary, Centennial Edition, Abridged Version

Copyright © 1990, 1978, 1974, 1963 by McGraw-Hill, Inc. All rights reserved. Copyright 1949
by McGraw-Hill, Inc. All rights reserved. Copyright renewed 1977. Printed in the United States
of America. Except as permitted under the United States Copyright Act of 1976, no part of this
publication may be reproduced or distributed in any form or by any means, or stored in a data
base or retrieval system, without the prior written permission of the publisher.

Send all inquiries to: Glencoe/McGraw-Hill, 936 Eastwind Drive,
Westerville, Ohio 43081

 2 3 4 5 6 7 8 9 10 11 12 13 14 15 — 00 99 98 97 96 95 94 93 92 91 90

ISBN 0-07-073682-0

FOREWORD

The *Gregg Shorthand Dictionary, Centennial Edition, Abridged Version,* is divided into five parts in order to provide maximum usefulness to writers who wish an authoritative outline for the most commonly used words, names, and phrases. The spiral binding assures ease of use.

CONTENTS

This dictionary contains words and phrases that students will encounter throughout the textbook materials and during dictation and transcription. The five parts contain the following listings:

Part 1 Words arranged in alphabetic order with the accompanying shorthand outlines.

Part 2 Brief forms and brief-form derivatives.

Part 3 Most frequently used phrases in business.

Part 4 Common names of men and women, as well as the most common surnames in the United States as compiled by the Social Security Administration.

Part 5 Geographic names, both American and foreign.

"DICTIONARY" OUTLINES

There is room for some difference of opinion as to the most appropriate outline for a given word. This dictionary offers outlines that have been discussed and decided upon by experienced writers of Gregg Shorthand. Sometimes an apparently obvious improvement in an outline will actually create the danger of a conflict in reading. More often, an outline different from the one provided in this dictionary would be individually satisfactory but would not be consistent with the outlines for other members of the same word family.

The publishers are confident that this dictionary will render a valuable service to shorthand writers by placing at their disposal a facile and fluent outline for almost any word, name, or phrase of interest to them.

PART 1

THEORY WORDS

A

a

aban•don

aban•don•ment

abase

abase•ment

abate

abate•ment

ab•bre•vi•ate

ab•bre•vi•at•ed

ab•bre•vi•a•tion

ab•di•cate

ab•di•ca•tion

ab•do•men

ab•dom•i•nal

ab•duct

ab•duc•tion

ab•er•ra•tion

abet

abet•ted

abey•ance

ab•hor

abide

abil•i•ties

abil•i•ty

able

ably

ab•nor•mal

ab•nor•mal•i•ty

aboard

abode

abol•ish

abol•ished

ab•o•li•tion

abom•i•nate

abound

about

above

abra•sion

abra•sive

abridge

ab•ro•gate

abrupt

ab•scess

ab•scond

ab•sent

ab•sen•tee

ab•sent•ly

ab•so•lute

ab•so•lute•ly

ab•solve

ab•sorb

ab•sorp•tion

ab•stain

ab•stract

ab•surd

abun•dance

abun•dant

abuse

abused

abyss

ac•a•dem•ic

acad•e•my

ac•cede

ac•cel•er•ate

ac•cel•er•a•tion

ac•cent

ac•cen•tu•ate

ac•cept

ac•cept•abil•i•ty

ac•cept•able

ac•cep•tance

ac•cept•ed

ac•cess

ac•ces•si•bil•i•ty

ac•ces•si•ble

ac•ces•so•ries

ac•ces•so•ry

ac•ci•dent

ac•ci•den•tal

ac•claim

ac•claimed

ac•com•mo•date

ac•com•mo•da•tion

ac•com•pa•nied

ac•com•pa•nies

ac•com•pa•ny

ac•com•plice

ac•com•plish

ac•com•plished

ac•com•plish•ment

ac•cord

ac•cor•dance

ac•cord•ed

ac•cord•ing•ly

ac•count

ac•count•abil•i•ty

ac•coun•tant

ac•cred•it

ac•cred•it•ed

ac•cru•al

ac•crue

ac•cru•ing

ac•cu•mu•late

ac•cu•mu•lat•ed

ac•cu•mu•la•tion

ac•cu•ra•cy

ac•cu•rate

ac•cu•rate•ly

ac•cuse

ac•cused

ac•cus•es

ac•cus•tom

ac•cus•tomed

ache

ached

achieve

achieved

achieve•ment

achieves

ac•knowl•edge

ac•knowl•edged

ac•knowl•edg•es

ac•knowl•edg•ment

ac•quaint

ac•quain•tance

ac•quaint•ed

ac•qui•esce

ac•qui•esced

ac•quire

ac•quired

ac•qui•si•tion

ac•quit

ac•quit•tal

across

act

act•ed

ac•tion

ac•ti•vate

ac•ti•vat•ed

ac•tive

ac•tive•ly

ac•tiv•ist

ac•tiv•i•ties

ac•tiv•i•ty

ac•tor

ac•tress

ac•tu•al

ac•tu•al•i•ty

ac•tu•al•ly

adapt

adapt•abil•i•ty

adapt•able

adapt•ed

add

add•ed

ad•den•dum

ad•dict

ad•dict•ed

ad•dic•tion

ad•di•tion

ad•di•tion•al

ad•di•tions

ad•dress

ad•dressed

ad•e•quate

ad•e•quate•ly

ad•here

ad•hered

ad•ja•cent

ad•jec•tive

ad•journ

ad•journ•ment

ad•junct

ad•just

ad•just•able

ad•just•ed

ad•just•ment

ad•justs

ad•min•is•ter

ad•min•is•tered

ad•min•is•tra•tive

ad•min•is•tra•tor

ad•mi•ra•ble

ad•mire

ad•mired

ad•mis•si•ble

ad•mis•sion

ad•mit

ad•mit•ted

ad•mit•ted•ly

ad•mon•ish

ad•o•les•cence

ad•o•les•cent

adopt

adopt•ed

adop•tion

ador•able

adore

adored

adorn

adorn•ment

ad•re•nal

adult

adult•hood

ad•vance

ad•vanced

ad•vance•ment

ad•vanc•es

ad•van•tage

ad•van•tag•es

ad•ven•ture

ad•verb

ad•verse

ad•verse•ly

ad•ver•si•ty

ad•ver•tise

ad•ver•tised

ad•ver•tise•ment

ad•ver•tis•er

ad•ver•tis•es

ad•vice

ad•vise

ad•vised

ad•vise•ment

ad•vis•es

ad•vi•so•ry

ad•vo•cate

aer•ate

ae•ri•al

aes•thet•ic

af•fect

af•fec•tion

af•fec•tion•ate

af•fec•tion•ate•ly

af•fi•da•vit

af•fil•i•ate

af•fil•i•a•tion

af•firm

af•fix

af•flict

af•flic•tion

af•flu•ent

af•ford

af•ford•ed

afore•thought

afraid

Af•ri•ca

af•ter

af•ter•noon

af•ter•thought

af•ter•ward

again

against

age

aged

agen•cies

agen•cy

agen•da

agent

ages

ag•gra•vate

ag•gre•gate

ag•grieve

aghast

ag•i•tate

ago

ag•o•nize

ag•o•ny

agree

agree•able

agreed

agree•ment

ag•ri•cul•ture

ahead

aid

ail•ment

aim

aimed

air

air•line

air•lines

air•mail

air•plane

air•port

aisle

alarm

alarmed

al•bum

al•co•hol

al•co•hol•ic

al•co•hol•ism

alert

al•i•bi

alien

alien•ate

align

align•ment

alike

al•i•mo•ny

alive

all

al•le•ga•tion

al•lege

al•le•giance

al•ler•gic

al•ler•gy

al•le•vi•ate

al•li•ance

al•lo•cate

al•lo•ca•tion

al•lot

al•lot•ment

al•lot•ted

al•low

al•low•able

al•low•ance

al•lowed

al•lows

al•lude

al•lure

al•ly

al•mighty

al•most

alone

along

aloud

al•pha•bet

al•pha•bet•ic

al•pha•bet•i•cal

al•pha•bet•ize

al•ready

al•so

al•tar

al•ter

al•ter•ation

al•tered

al•ter•nate

al•ter•na•tive

al•ter•na•tor

al•though

al•ti•tude

al•to•geth•er

al•tru•is•tic

alu•mi•num

alum•na

alum•nae

alum•ni

alum•nus

al•ways

am ——

am•a•teur

amaze

amaz•ing•ly

am•bas•sa•dor

am•bi•dex•trous

am•bi•gu•ity

am•big•u•ous

am•bi•tion

am•bi•tious

am•biv•a•lence

am•biv•a•lent

am•bu•lance

amend

amend•ment

Amer•i•can

ami•a•ble

amidst

am•ne•sia

am•nes•ty

among

am•or•tize

amount

amount•ed

am•pi•cil•lin

am•ple

am•pli•fy

am•pu•tate

am•pu•ta•tion

am•pu•tee

Am•trak

amuse

amused

amuse•ment

amus•es

an

an•al•ge•sic

anal•o•gy

anal•y•sis

an•a•lyst

an•a•lyt•i•cal

an•a•lyze

an•a•lyzed

an•ar•chist

an•ar•chy

anat•o•my

an•ces•tor

an•chor

an•chored

an•cient

and

an•es•the•sia

an•es•the•sis

an•es•thet•ic

an•gel

an•ger

an•gle

an•gry

an•guish

an•i•mal

an•i•mos•i•ty

an•kle

an•nex

an•nex•ation

an•nexed

an•ni•hi•late

an•ni•ver•sa•ries

an•ni•ver•sa•ry

an•no•tate

an•nounce

an•nounced

an•nounce•ment

an•nounc•es

an•noy

an•noy•ance

an•noyed

an•nu•al

an•nu•al•ly

anoint

anon•y•mous

an•swer

an•swered

ant

ant•ac•id

an•tag•o•nism

an•tag•o•nist

an•tag•o•nize

an•ten•na

an•thol•o•gy

an•thro•pol•o•gy

an•ti•body

an•tic

an•tic•i•pate

an•tic•i•pat•ed

an•tic•i•pa•tion

an•ti•cli•max

an•ti•dote

an•tique

an•ti•trust

anx•i•ety

anx•ious

anx•ious•ly

any

any•body

any•how

any•one

any•thing

any•time

any•way

any•where

aor•ta

apart

apart•ment

ap•a•thy

apol•o•get•ic

apol•o•gies

apol•o•gize

apol•o•gized

apol•o•gy

apos•tro•phe

ap•palled

ap•pa•ra•tus

ap•par•el

ap•par•ent

ap•par•ent•ly

ap•peal

ap•pealed

ap•pear

ap•pear•ance

ap•pease

ap•pel•lant

ap•pel•late

ap•pend•age

ap•pen•dec•to•my

ap•pen•di•ci•tis

ap•pen•dix

ap•pe•tite

ap•plaud

ap•plause

ap•ple

ap•pli•ance

ap•pli•anc•es

ap•pli•ca•ble

ap•pli•cant

ap•pli•ca•tion

ap•plied

ap•ply

ap•point

ap•point•ed

ap•point•ment

ap•po•si•tion

ap•prais•al

ap•praise

ap•pre•cia•ble

ap•pre•ci•ate

ap•pre•ci•at•ed

ap•pre•ci•a•tion

ap•pre•hend

ap•pre•hen•sion

ap•pre•hen•sive

ap•pren•tice

ap•prise

ap•proach

ap•proached

ap•pro•pri•ate

ap•pro•pri•at•ed

ap•pro•pri•ate•ly

ap•pro•pri•ate•ness

ap•pro•pri•a•tion

ap•prov•al

ap•prove

ap•proved

ap•prov•ing•ly

ap•prox•i•mate

ap•prox•i•mate•ly

ap•prox•i•ma•tion

April

apt

ap•ti•tude

aquar•i•um

aquat•ic

Arab

ar•bi•trary

ar•bi•trate

ar•cade

arch

ar•chae•ol•o•gy

ar•cha•ic

ar•chi•tect

ar•du•ous

are

ar•ea

ar•eas

are•na

ar•gue

ar•gu•ment

ar•gu•men•ta•tive

arise

ar•is•toc•ra•cy

aris•to•crat

arith•me•tic

ar•ith•met•i•cal

ar•mor

ar•my

around

arouse

ar•raign

ar•raign•ment

ar•range

ar•ranged

ar•range•ment

ar•rang•es

ar•rest

ar•riv•al

ar•rive

ar•rived

ar•ro•gance

ar•ro•gant

ar•ro•gate

ar•row

ar•se•nic

ar•son

art

ar•tery

ar•thri•tis

ar•ti•cle

ar•ti•cles

ar•tic•u•late

ar•ti•fi•cial

art•ist

ar•tis•tic

art•ists

art•work

as

as•cend

as•cer•tain

Asia

Asian

as•i•nine

ask

asked

asleep

as•pect

as•phyx•i•ate

as•pi•ra•tion

as•pire

as•pi•rin

as•sail•ant

as•sas•sin

as•sas•si•nate

as•sault

as•sault•ed

as•sem•ble

as•sem•blies

as•sem•bly

as•sent

as•sert

as•sert•ed

as•ser•tion

as•ser•tive

as•sess

as•sessed

as•sess•ment

as•set

as•sets

as•sign

as•signed

as•sign•ment

as•sim•i•late

as•sist

as•sis•tance

as•sis•tant

as•sist•ed

as•so•ciate

as•sort

as•sort•ed

as•sort•ment

as•sume

as•sumed

as•sure

as•sured

asth•ma

asth•mat•ic

as•ton•ish

as•ton•ish•ing•ly

as•ton•ish•ment

as•tound

astray

as•trol•o•gy

as•tro•naut

as•tron•o•mer

as•tron•o•my

as•tute•ly

as•tute•ness

asy•lum

at

ate

ath•lete

ath•let•ic

at•mo•sphere

at•om

atom•ic

atro•cious

atroc•i•ty

at•tach

at•tached

at•tach•ment

at•tack

at•tain

at•tained

at•tempt

at•tempt•ed

at•tend

at•ten•dance

at•ten•dant

at•tend•ed

at•ten•tion

at•ten•tive

at•ten•u•ate

at•tic

at•tire

at•ti•tude

at•tor•ney

at•tor•neys

at•tract

at•tract•ed

at•trac•tion

at•trib•ute

at•trib•ut•ed

au•burn

auc•tion

auc•tion•eer

au•dac•i•ty

au•di•ble

au•di•ence

au•dio•vi•su•al

au•dit

au•dit•ed

au•di•tor

au•di•to•ri•um

aug•ment

aug•ment•ed

Au•gust

aunt

aus•pi•cious

aus•tere

au•then•tic

au•then•ti•cate

au•then•tic•i•ty

au•thor

au•thor•i•ties

au•thor•i•ty

au•tho•ri•za•tion

au•tho•rize

au•tho•rized

au•thors

au•thor•ship

au•to

au•to•bi•og•ra•phy

au•to•crat

au•to•crat•ic

au•to•graph

au•to•mat•ic

au•to•ma•tion

au•to•mo•bile

au•ton•o•mous

au•ton•o•my

au•top•sy

au•tumn

avail

avail•abil•i•ty

avail•able

availed

av•a•rice

avenge

av•e•nue

av•er•age

av•er•aged

aver•sion

avoid

avoid•able

avoid•ed

await

await•ed

awaits

awake

awak•en

award

award•ed

awards

aware

away

ax

ax•i•om

ax•is

ax•le

B

ba•by

bach•e•lor

back

back•ache

back•bone

back•ground

back•up

back•ward

back•wards

bac•te•ria

bad

bad•ly

bag

bag•gage

bai•liff

bail•ment

bait

bake

bak•er

bak•ery

bal•ance

bal•anced

bal•co•ny

bald

bale

ball

bal•let

bal•lot

ball•room

band

ban•dage

ban•dy

bang

ban•ish

bank

bank•book

banked

bank•er

bank•rupt

bank•rupt•cy

ban•quet

bap•tism

bap•tize

bar

bar•ber

bare•ly

bar•gain

bar•gains

bark

base

based

base•ment

ba•si•cal•ly

ba•sin

ba•sis

bas•ket

bas•ket•ball

bass

bat

bath

bath•room

bat•ter

bat•tery

bat•tle

bay

be

beach

bea•con

bead

bead•ed

bea•gle

beam

bean

bear

beard

beast

beat

beau•ti•ful

beau•ti•ful•ly

beau•ty

be•came

be•cause

be•come

bed

bed•room

bee

beef

been

beer

be•fore

be•fore•hand

be•gan

beg•gar

be•gin

be•gin•ner

be•go•nia

be•guile

be•gun

be•half

be•have

be•hav•ior

be•hind

be•hold

beige

be•lat•ed

Bel•gian

be•lief

be•lieve

be•lieved

bel•lig•er•ence

bel•lig•er•ent

be•long

be•longed

be•long•ings

be•longs

be•loved

be•low

belt

bench

bend

be•neath

bene•fac•tor

be•nef•i•cent

ben•e•fi•cial

ben•e•fi•cia•ry

ben•e•fit

ben•e•fit•ed

be•nev•o•lent

be•nign

be•quest

be•side

be•siege

best

bet	bio•graph•i•cal	blind
be•tray	bi•og•ra•phy	blind•ly
bet•ter	bi•o•log•i•cal	blink
be•tween	bi•ol•o•gy	bliss
bev•er•age	bio•rhythm	blis•ter
bevy	bird	blithe
be•ware	birth	bliz•zard
be•yond	birth•day	block
bi•an•nu•al	bis•cuit	blood
bi•as	bisque	blood•line
bi•cy•cle	bite	bloom
bid	bit•ter	blos•som
big	bit•ter•ness	blown
big•ger	bi•zarre	blow•out
big•gest	black•mail	blue
big•ot	blad•der	bluff
bill	blame	blun•der
bill•board	blamed	blunt
billed	bland	blush
bill•ings	blank	board
bil•lion	blan•ket	boast
bil•lion•aire	blast	boat
bi•month•ly	bleach	bodi•ly
bind	bleed	body
bind•ings	blend	body•guard
bin•oc•u•lar	bless	boil
bio•graph•ic	blew	bois•ter•ous

bold

bolt

bomb

bom•bard

bond

bond•ed

bonds

bone

book

booked

book•keep•ing

book•let

book•lets

books

book•store

boom

boost

boot

bor•der

bore

bore•dom

bor•ing

bor•row

bor•rowed

boss

bo•tan•i•cal

both

both•er

both•ered

bot•tle

bot•tom

bought

bouil•lon

bou•le•vard

bounce

bound

bound•ary

boun•ti•ful

bou•quet

bour•geois

bour•geoi•sie

box

boxed

box•es

boy

boy•hood

boys

brace

brac•es

brack•et

braille

brain

braise

branch

brand

brass

brave

breach

bread

breadth

break

break•down

break•fast

break•out

break•through

break•up

breast

breath

breech

breed

breeze

brev•i•ty

brew

bribe

brib•ery

bride

bride•groom

brides•maid

bridge

brief

brief•case

brief•ly	broth•er•hood	buri•al
bright•en	broth•er-in-law	burn•out
bril•liance	broth•er•ly	bur•sar
bril•liant	brought	bur•si•tis
bring	browse	bus
bri•oche	brunch	bus•es
brisk	brush	bush
brisk•ly	brusque	busi•ness
Brit•ish	bru•tal	busi•ness•es
broad	buck•le	busi•ness•like
broad•cast	bud	busi•ness•man
broad•en	budge	busi•ness•men
broad•ly	bud•get	busi•ness•wom•an
broad•way	bud•get•ary	busi•ness•wom•en
bro•cade	bud•get•ed	
broc•co•li	buf•fet	bust
bro•chure	build	busy
broil	build•er	but
broke	build•ings	but•ler
bro•ken	bulb	but•ter
bro•ker	bull	but•ton
bro•ker•age	bul•le•tin	buy
bron•chi•tis	bur•den	buy•er
bronze	bur•den•some	buz•zard
brook	bu•reau	by
broom	bu•reau•cra•cy	by•pass
broth•er	bu•reau•crat	by-prod•uct

C

cab•i•net

ca•ble

ca•ble•gram

cac•ti

cac•tus

cad•re

ca•fé

caf•e•te•ria

caf•feine

cage

ca•jole

cake

ca•lam•i•ty

cal•ci•um

cal•cu•late

cal•cu•lat•ed

cal•cu•la•tion

cal•cu•la•tions

cal•cu•la•tor

cal•en•dar

cal•i•ber

call

called

cal•lig•ra•phy

cal•lous

calm

calm•ly

cal•o•rie

came

cam•era

cam•i•sole

cam•ou•flage

camp

cam•paign

cam•pus

can

can•cel

can•celed

can•cel•la•tion

can•cer

can•did

can•dle

can•dor

cane

ca•nine

can•not

ca•noe

can•on

can•tan•ker•ous

can•vas

can•vass

ca•pa•bil•i•ties

ca•pa•bil•i•ty

ca•pa•ble

ca•pac•i•tate

ca•pac•i•ty

cap•i•tal

cap•i•tal•ism

cap•i•tal•ist

cap•i•tal•iza•tion

cap•i•tal•ize

cap•i•tol

ca•pit•u•late

cap•tain

cap•ti•vate

cap•tive

cap•ture

car

car•bo•hy•drate

car•bon

car•bon•ate

car•cin•o•gen•ic

card

car•di•ac

car•di•ol•o•gy

cared

ca•reer

care•free

care•ful

care•ful•ly

care•less

care•less•ly

car•go

car•pet

car•riage

car•ried

car•ries

car•ry

car•ton

car•toon

carve

cas•es

cash

cash•ier

cas•se•role

cas•sette

cast

cas•tle

ca•su•al

ca•su•al•ly

ca•su•al•ties

cat

cat•a•log

cat•a•loged

cat•a•logs

cat•a•lyst

cat•a•ract

ca•tas•tro•phe

catch

catch•es

cat•e•go•ry

ca•ter

ca•the•dral

cath•o•lic

cat•tle

cau•li•flow•er

cause

caused

caus•es

cau•tion

cau•tioned

cau•tious

cave

ca•ve•at

cav•i•ar

cav•i•ty

cease

ceased

ceas•es

cel•e•brate

cen•sor•ship

cen•sus

cent

cen•ten•ni•al

cen•ter

cen•tral

cen•tral•iza•tion

cen•tral•ize

cer•ti•fi•ca•tion

cer•ti•fy

cer•tio•ra•ri

chain

chair

chair•per•son

change

changed

chang•es

chan•nel

chan•neled

cha•os

chap•el

chap•ter

char•ac•ter

char•ac•ter•is•tic

cha•rade

charge

charg•es

cha•ris•ma

char•i•ties

char·i·ty

chart

char·ter

chase

chasm

chaste

chas·tise

châ·teau

chat·ter

chauf·feur

chau·vin·ism

chau·vin·ist

cheap

cheap·er

cheat

check

check·book

checked

checks

cheer

cheer·ful

cheer·ful·ly

cheese

chem·i·cal

chem·i·cal·ly

chem·i·cals

chem·ist

chem·is·try

cher·ish

chest

chew

chick·en

chief

child

child·hood

child·ish

child·like

chil·dren

chill

chi·na

chi·ro·prac·tor

chlo·ride

chlo·rine

chlo·ro·phyll

choc·o·late

choice

choir

choose

cho·rus

chose

cho·sen

chow·der

chris·ten

Chris·tian

Christ·mas

chrome

chron·ic

chron·i·cle

chro·no·log·i·cal

chro·nol·o·gy

church

ci·gar

cig·a·rette

cin·e·ma

cin·na·mon

cir·cle

cir·cled

cir·cuit

cir·cu·lar

cir·cu·lars

cir·cu·late

cir·cu·lat·ed

cir·cu·la·tion

cir·cum·scribe

cir·cum·spect

cir·cum·stance

cir·cum·stanc·es

cir·cum·stan·tial

cir·cum·vent

ci·ta·tion

cite

cit•ed

cit•ies

cit•i•zen

cit•i•zen•ship

city

civ•il

civ•i•lize

claim

claimed

clap

clar•i•fi•ca•tion

clar•i•ty

class

class•es

clas•sic

clas•si•cal

clas•si•fi•ca•tion

clas•si•fy

class•room

class•work

clause

clean

cleanse

cleans•er

clean•up

clear

clear•ly

cler•i•cal

clerk

clev•er

cli•ent

cli•en•tele

cli•mate

climb

clin•ic

clin•i•cal

clip

clock

clock•wise

clois•ter

close

clos•er

close•ly

clos•et

cloth

clothes

cloud

cloudy

clown

club

clum•sy

clus•ter

coach

coal

coarse

coast

coast•al

coat

coax

co•balt

co•caine

co•coa

co•co•nut

code

co•de•fen•dant

cod•i•cil

co•ed

co•ed•u•ca•tion

co•ef•fi•cient

co•erce

co•er•cion

co•er•cive

co•ex•ec•u•tor

cof•fee

cof•fin

cog•ni•tion

cog•ni•zant

co•hab•it

co•her•ent

co•he•sive

coin

co•in•cide

co•in•ci•dence

co•in•ci•den•tal

coke

cold

col•i•se•um

col•lab•o•rate

col•lab•o•ra•tion

col•lage

col•lapse

col•lar

col•late

col•lat•er•al

col•league

col•lect

col•lect•ible

col•lec•tion

col•lege

col•le•giate

col•lide

col•li•sion

co•lon

col•o•nel

co•lo•nial

col•o•ny

col•or

col•umn

com•bat

com•bi•na•tion

com•bine

com•bined

come

co•me•di•an

com•e•dy

com•fort

com•fort•able

com•fort•ably

com•fort•ed

com•ic

com•i•cal

com•ma

com•mand

com•mand•ed

com•mand•ment

com•mem•o•rate

com•mence

com•menced

com•mence•ment

com•mend

com•mend•able

com•mend•ed

com•ment

com•men•tary

com•ment•ed

com•merce

com•mer•cial

com•min•gle

com•mis•sion

com•mis•sion•er

com•mit

com•mit•ment

com•mit•ted

com•mit•tee

com•mit•tees

com•mod•i•ty

com•mon

com•mon•ly

com•mon•wealth

com•mu•ni•cate

com•mu•ni•cat•ed

com•mu•ni•ca•tion

com•mu•ni•ca•tions

com•mu•nism

com•mu•nist

com•mu•ni•ty

com•mute

com•pact

com•pa•nies

com•pan•ion

com•pan•ion•ship

com•pa•ny

com•pa•ra•ble

com•pare

com•pared

com•par•i•son

com•pass

com•pas•sion

com•pat•i•bil•i•ty

com•pat•i•ble

com•pel

com•pelled

com•pel•ling•ly

com•pen•sate

com•pen•sat•ed

com•pen•sa•tion

com•pete

com•pet•ed

com•pe•tence

com•pe•ten•cy

com•pe•tent

com•pe•ti•tion

com•pet•i•tive

com•pet•i•tor

com•pile

com•piled

com•pla•cen•cy

com•pla•cent

com•plain

com•plained

com•plaint

com•ple•ment

com•ple•men•ta•ry

com•plete

com•plet•ed

com•plete•ly

com•ple•tion

com•plex

com•plex•ion

com•plex•i•ty

com•pli•ance

com•pli•ant

com•pli•cate

com•pli•ca•tion

com•pli•ment

com•pli•men•ta•ry

com•pli•ment•ed

com•ply

com•po•nent

com•pose

com•posed

com•pos•er

com•pos•es

com•pos•ite

com•pos•i•tor

com•po•sure

com•pound

com•pre•hend

com•pre•hen•sion

com•pre•hen•sive

com•press

com•pres•sion

com•prise

com•prised

com•pro•mise

com•pul•sive

com•pul•so•ry

com•pute

com•put•ed

com•put•er

com•put•er•ized

com•rade

con•ceal

con•ceit

con•ceiv•able

con•ceiv•ably

con•ceive

con•cen•trate

con•cen•tra•tion

con•cept

con•cep•tion

con•cep•tu•al

con•cern

con•cerned

con•cert

con•clude

con•clud•ed

con•clu•sion

con•clu•sive

con•coct

con•crete

con•cur

con•curred

con•cur•rence

con•cur•rent

con•demn

con•demned

con•dense

con•dens•es

con•de•scend

con•di•tion

con•di•tion•al

con•duct

con•duct•ed

con•fer

con•fer•ence

con•fer•en•ces

con•fess

con•fes•sion

con•fide

con•fi•dence

con•fi•dent

con•fi•den•tial

con•fi•dent•ly

con•firm

con•fir•ma•tion

con•firmed

con•fis•cate

con•flict

con•flict•ed

con•form

con•formed

con•for•mi•ty

con•front

con•fuse

con•fu•sion

con•ge•nial

con•glom•er•ate

con•grat•u•late

con•grat•u•lat•ed

con•grat•u•la•tion

con•grat•u•la•to•ry

con•gre•gate

con•gress

con•gres•sio•nal

co•ni•fer

con•jec•ture

con•junc•tion

con•jure

con•nect

con•nect•ed

con•nec•tion

con•nois•seur

con•quer

con•quest

con•science

con•sci•en•tious

con•scious

con•scious•ly

con•sec•u•tive

con•sen•sus

con•sent

con•se•quence

con•se•quenc•es

con•se•quent

con•se•quent•ly

con•serve

con•sid•er

con•sid•er•able

con•sid•er•ably

con•sid•er•ate

con•sid•er•ation

con•sist

con•sist•ed

con•sis•ten•cy

con•sis•tent

con•so•la•tion

con•sol•i•date

con•spic•u•ous

con•spir•a•cy

con•stant

con•stant•ly

con•stel•la•tion

con•sti•pa•tion

con•stit•u•ent

con•sti•tute

con•sti•tut•ed

con•sti•tu•tion

con•sti•tu•tion•al

con•struct

con•strue

con•sul•ate

con•sult

con•sul•tant

con•sult•ed

con•sume

con•sump•tion

con•tact

con•tain

con•tained

con•tam•i•nate

con•tem•plate

con•tem•po•rary

con•tempt

con•tempt•ible

con•tend

con•ten•tion

con•tent

con•tent•ment

con•test

con•text

con•tig•u•ous

con•ti•nent

con•ti•nen•tal

con•tin•gen•cy

con•tin•gent

con•tin•u•al

con•tin•ue

con•tin•ued

con•tin•ues

con•tin•u•ous

con•tin•u•ous•ly

con•tor•tion

con•tour

con•tract

con•trac•tion

con•trac•tu•al

con•tra•dict

con•trary

con•trast

con•trib•ute

con•trib•ut•ed

con•tri•bu•tion

con•tri•bu•tions

con•trol

con•trolled

con•tro•ver•sial

con•tro•ver•sy

con•va•lesce

con•va•les•cence

con•va•les•cent

con•vene

con•ve•nience

con•ve•nienc•es

con•ve•nient

con•ve•nient•ly

con•ven•tion

con•ven•tion•al

con•verge

con•ver•sa•tion

con•ver•sion

con•vert

con•vert•ible

con•vex

con•vey

con•vey•ance

con•veyed

con•vict

con•vict•ed

con•vic•tion

con•vince

con•vinced

con•vul•sion

cook•book

co•op•er•ate

co•op•er•at•ed

co•op•er•a•tion

co•op•er•a•tive

co•or•di•nate

cop•ied

copi•er

cop•ies

cop•per

copy

copy•hold•er

copy•right

cor•al

cor•dial

cor•dial•ly

core

co•re•spon•dent

corn

cor•ner

cor•o•nary

cor•po•ral

cor•po•rate

cor•po•ra•tion

cor•rect

cor•rec•tion

cor•rec•tions

cor•rect•ly

cor•re•late

cor•re•spond

cor•re•spond•ed

cor•re•spon•dence

cor•re•spon•dent

cor•re•spon•dents

cor•re•spond•ing•ly

cor•re•sponds

cor•rupt

cor•tex

cos•met•ic

cos•mo•pol•i•tan

cost

cost•ly

cos•tume

cot•tage

cot•ton

could

coun•cil

coun•sel

coun•seled

count

count•er

coun•ter•bal•ance

coun•ter•feit

coun•tries

coun•try

coun•ty

cou•ple

cour•age

cou•ra•geous

course

cours•es

court

court•ed

cour•te•ous

cour•te•sy

court•yard

cous•in

cov•er

cov•er•age

cov•ered

cow•ard

co-work•er

coy

crack

craft

cramp

cra•ni•um

crank

crate

crave

crawl

cra•zy

cream

cre•ate

cre•at•ed

cre•ation

cre•ative

cre•ativ•i•ty

crea•ture

cre•den•tial

cred•i•bil•i•ty

cred•it

cred•it•abil•i•ty

cred•it•able

cred•it•ed

cred•i•tor

cred•u•lous

creed

cre•mate

crepe

crest

crev•ice

crib

crime

crim•i•nal

crim•i•nol•o•gy

crim•son

cringe

cri•ses

cri•sis

cri•te•ria

crit•ic

crit•i•cal

crit•i•cism

crit•i•cize

cri•tique

crook

crop

cross

cross•road

cross•walk

cross•word

crow

crowd

cru•cial

cru•ci•fy

crude

cru•el

cru•el•ty

cruise

cru•sade

crush

cry

crys•tal

cu•bic

cu•bi•cle

cue

cui•sine

cul•mi•nate

cul•ti•vate

cul•tur•al

cul•ture

cup

cup•ful

cure

cu•ri•os•i•ty

cu•ri•ous

cu•ri•ous•ly

curl

cur•ren•cy

cur•rent

cur•rent•ly

cur•ric•u•lum

curse

cur•so•ry

cur•tail

cur•tain

curve

cush•ion

cus•to•di•an

cus•to•dy

cus•tom•ari•ly

cus•tom•er

cus•tom•ers

cus•toms

cut

cut•let

cy•cle

cyl•in•der

cyn•ic

cyn•i•cal

czar

D

dad

dai•ly

dairy

dai•sy

dam

dam•age

dam•aged

dam•ag•es

dammed

damp

damp•en

dance

danc•er

dan•ger

dan•ger•ous

dan•ger•ous•ly

dare

dark

dark•ness

dar•ling

dart

dash

da•ta

date

dat•ed

da•tum

daugh•ter

daugh•ter-in-law

dawn

day

day•light

days

day•time

dea•con

dead

dead•line

dead•ly

deaf

deal

deal•er

deal•ings

dear

dear•ly

death

de•ba•cle

de•bate

de•bat•ed

deb•it

deb•it•ed

debt

debt•or

de•cade

de•cap•i•tate

de•cay

de•cease

de•ceased

de•ceit

De•cem•ber

de•cent

de•cen•tral•iza•tion

de•cen•tral•ize

de•cep•tion

de•cep•tive

de•cide

de•cid•ed

dec•i•mal

de•ci•sion

de•ci•sive

deck

dec•la•ra•tion

de•clare

de•cline

de•com•pose

dec•o•rate

dec•o•ra•tion

dec•o•ra•tor

de•crease

de•creased

de•cree

de•crep•it

ded•i•cate

de•duce

de•duced

de•duct

de•duct•ed

de•duct•ible

de•duc•tion

deed

deem

deemed

deep

deep•ly

deer

de-es•ca•late

de•fam•a•to•ry

de•fault

de•feat

de•fend

de•fen•dant

de•fense

de•fens•es

de•fen•sive

de•fer

def•er•en•tial

de•fer•ment

de•ferred

de•fi•ant

de•fi•cien•cy

de•fi•cient

def•i•cit

de•fine

de•fined

def•i•nite

def•i•nite•ly

def•i•ni•tion

de•flate

de•flect

de•form

de•formed

de•for•mi•ty

de•fraud

de•fray

de•frost

deft

de•fy

de•grade

de•gree

de•ject•ed

de•lay

de•lec•ta•ble

del•e•gate

del•e•ga•tion

de•lete

de•le•tion

de•lib•er•ate

del•i•cate

del•i•ca•tes•sen

de•li•cious

de•light

de•light•ed

de•light•ful

de•lin•eate

de•lin•quent

de•liv•er

de•liv•ery

de•lude

de•lu•sion

de•mand

de•mean

de•mean•or

de•mise

de•moc•ra•cy

dem•o•crat

de•mol•ish

de•mon

dem•on•strate

dem•on•stra•tion

de•mure

de•mur•rer

de•ni•al

de•nied

de•nies

de•nom•i•na•tion

de•note

de•nounce

den•si•ty

den•tal

den•tist

de•ny

de•part

de•part•ed

de•part•ment

de•part•men•tal

de•pend

de•pend•abil•i•ty

de•pend•able

de•pen•den•cy

de•pen•dent

de•pict

de•plete

de•plore

de•ploy

de•port

de•por•ta•tion

de•port•ment

de•pos•it

de•pos•it•ed

de•pos•it•or

de•pos•i•to•ry

dep•re•cate

de•pre•ci•ate

de•pre•ci•a•tion

de•pres•sion

de•prive

depth

dep•u•ty

de•range

der•e•lict

der•i•va•tion

de•riv•a•tive

de•rive

der•ma•ti•tis

der•ma•tol•o•gy

de•scribe

de•scrip•tion

des•e•crate

des•ert

de•sert

de•serve

de•sign

des•ig•nate

de•signed

de•sir•abil•i•ty

de•sir•able

de•sire

de•sired

de•sires

desk

desks

des•o•late

de•spair

des•per•ate

des•per•a•tion

de•spise

de•spite

de•spon•dent

des•pot

des•sert

des•ti•na•tion

des•ti•ny

de•stroy

de•tach

de•tail

de•tailed

de•tain

de•tect

de•te•ri•o•rate

de•ter•mi•na•tion

de•ter•mine

de•test

de•tour

de•tract

de•trac•tion

det•ri•ment

de•vel•op

de•vel•oped

de•vel•op•ment

de•vi•ate

de•vice

de•vi•ous

de•vise

de•vis•es

de•void

de•vote

de•vot•ed

de•vo•tion

de•vour

de•voured

dex•ter•i•ty

dex•ter•ous

di•a•be•tes

di•a•bet•ic

di•ag•nose

di•ag•no•sis

di•a•gram

di•al

di•a•lect

di•a•logue

di•al•y•sis

di•a•mond

di•a•phragm

di•a•ry

di•chot•o•my

dic•tate

dic•ta•tion

dic•ta•tor

dic•tion

dic•tio•nary

did

die

di•et

dif•fer

dif•fer•ence

dif•fer•enc•es

dif•fer•ent

dif•fer•en•ti•ate

dif•fer•en•ti•a•tion

dif•fi•cult

dif•fi•cul•ties

dif•fi•cul•ty

dif•fuse

di•gest

di•ges•tion

dig•it

dig•ni•fy

dig•ni•ty

di•gress

di•late

di•lem•ma

dil•i•gence

dil•i•gent

di•lute

dim

dime

di•men•sion

di•min•ish

din•er

din•ner

di•no•saur

di•o•cese

di•plo•ma

dip•lo•mat

di•rect

di•rect•ed

di•rec•tion

di•rec•tion•al

di•rect•ly

di•rec•tor

di•rec•to•ry

dirt

dis•abil•i•ty

dis•able

dis•abled

dis•ad•van•tage

dis•ad•van•ta•geous

dis•af•firm

dis•agree

dis•agree•able

dis•agree•ment

dis•al•low

dis•ap•pear

dis•ap•pear•ance

dis•ap•point

dis•ap•point•ment

dis•ap•prov•al

dis•ap•prove

dis•ar•ray

di•sas•ter

di•sas•trous

dis•bar

dis•burse

dis•burse•ment

disc

dis•card

dis•cern

dis•cern•ible

dis•charge

dis•ci•ple

dis•ci•pline

dis•close

dis•clo•sure

dis•com•fort

dis•con•tent

dis•con•tin•ue

dis•con•tin•ues

dis•count

dis•cour•age

dis•cour•age•ment

dis•cour•te•ous

dis•cov•er

dis•cred•it

dis•creet

dis•crete

dis•cre•tion

dis•cre•tion•ary

dis•crim•i•na•tion

dis•cuss

dis•cussed

dis•cus•sion

dis•dain

dis•ease

dis•eased

dis•grace

dis•guise

dis•gust

dish

dis•hon•est

dis•hon•or

dis•in•fect

disk

dis•like

dis•lo•cate

dis•mal

dis•may

dis•miss

dis•miss•al

dis•obe•di•ence

dis•obe•di•ent

dis•obey

dis•or•der

dis•or•dered

dis•or•der•ly

dis•or•ga•nize

dis•own

dis•patch

dis•pel

dis•pens•able

dis•pense

dis•perse

dis•place

dis•play

dis•please

dis•pose

dis•pute

dis•qual•i•fy

dis•re•gard

dis•rupt

dis•rup•tion

dis•rup•tive

dis•sat•is•fied

dis•sect

dis•sim•i•lar

dis•si•pate

dis•solve

dis•suade

dis•tance

dis•tant

dis•till

dis•tinct

dis•tinc•tion

dis•tinct•ly

dis•tin•guish

dis•tort

dis•tract

dis•tress

dis•trib•ute

dis•tri•bu•tion

dis•trib•u•tor

dis•trict

dis•trust

dis•turb

dis•tur•bance

dit•to

di•verge

di•ver•gence

di•verse

di•ver•si•fi•ca•tion

di•ver•si•fy

di•ver•sion

di•ver•si•ty

di•vert

di•vest

di•vide

div•i•dend

di•vine

di•vi•sion

di•vorce

di•vorced

di•vor•cée

di•vulge

do

doc•ile

doc•tor

doc•tor•ate

doc•trine

doc•u•ment

doc•u•men•ta•ry

doc•u•men•ta•tion

does

doesn't

dog•ma

dol•lar

do•main

dome

do•mes•tic

dom•i•nance

dom•i•nant

dom•i•nate

dom•i•na•tion

do•nate

do•na•tion

done

do•nor

door

dos•age

dose

dou•ble

doubt

doubt•ed

doubt•ful

doubt•less

dough

down

down•fall

down•town

down•ward

dow•ry

doz•en

Dr.

draft

draft•ed

drain

dra•ma

dra•mat•ic

drank

dras•tic

draw

draw•ee

draw•er

draw•ings

dread

dread•ful

dream

dress

drew

drift

drill

drink

drive

driv•en

drop

drop•out

drove

drown

drowsy

drug

drug•store

drum

drunk

dry

dry•er

du•al

duct

due

dues

dull

du•ly

dumb

du•pli•cate

du•pli•ca•tion

du•ra•bil•i•ty

du•ra•ble

dur•ing

dust

E

dust mop	each	echo
dust storm	ea•ger	eclipse
dusty	ea•ger•ly	ecol•o•gy
du•ties	ear	eco•nom•ic
du•ti•ful	ear•ache	eco•nom•i•cal
du•ty	ear•li•er	econ•o•mist
dwell	ear•li•est	econ•o•my
dwell•ings	ear•ly	ec•sta•sy
dwin•dle	earn	ec•stat•ic
dye	earned	ec•ze•ma
dy•nam•ic	ear•nest	edge
dy•na•mite	ear•nest•ly	ed•it
dy•nas•ty	earn•ings	ed•it•ed
dys•lex•ic	earth	edi•tion
	eas•i•er	ed•i•tor
	eas•i•est	ed•i•to•ri•al
	eas•i•ly	ed•u•cate
	east	ed•u•ca•tion
	east•ern	ed•u•ca•tion•al
	east•ward	ef•fect
	easy	ef•fec•tive
	eat	ef•fer•ves•cence
	eat•en	ef•fer•ves•cent
	eb•o•ny	ef•fi•ca•cy
	ec•cen•tric	ef•fi•cien•cy
		ef•fi•cient
		ef•fi•cient•ly

ef•fort

ego

ego•cen•tric

ego•tis•tic

ei•ther

eject

ejec•tion

elab•o•rate

elapse

elapsed

elas•tic

elate

el•der

el•der•ly

elect

elec•tion

elec•tive

elec•tric

elec•tri•cal

elec•tri•cian

elec•tric•i•ty

elec•tri•fy

elec•tron

elec•tron•ic

elec•tron•ics

el•e•gance

el•e•gant

el•e•ment

el•e•men•ta•ry

el•e•vate

el•e•va•tor

elic•it

el•i•gi•ble

elim•i•nate

elim•i•na•tion

elite

elm

elope

el•o•quent

el•o•quent•ly

else•where

em•a•nate

eman•ci•pate

em•balm

em•bar•rass

em•bar•rassed

em•bar•rass•ment

em•bas•sy

em•bez•zle

em•blem

em•body

em•boss

em•brace

em•bryo

emerge

emer•gence

emer•gen•cy

em•i•grant

emis•sion

emo•tion

emo•tion•al

emo•tions

em•per•or

em•pha•size

em•phat•ic

em•pire

em•ploy

em•ploy•ee

em•ploy•ees

em•ploy•er

em•ploy•ment

em•pow•er

emp•tied

emp•ti•ness

emp•ty

em•u•late

emul•si•fy

emul•sion

en•able

en•abled

en•act

en•act•ment

en•chant

en•chant•ment

en•close

en•closed

en•clos•es

en•clo•sure

en•coun•ter

en•cour•age

en•cour•age•ment

en•cum•ber

end

en•dear

en•deav•or

end•ings

end•less

en•dorse

en•dorse•ment

en•dors•es

en•dow•ment

en•dur•able

en•dur•ance

en•dure

en•e•my

en•er•get•ic

en•er•gize

en•er•gy

en•force

en•force•able

en•forced

en•force•ment

en•gage

en•gage•ment

en•gine

en•gi•neer

En•glish

en•grave

en•gross

en•hance

en•joy

en•joy•able

en•joy•ment

en•large

en•large•ment

en•light•en

en•light•ened

en•light•en•ment

en•list

en•list•ment

enor•mous

enough

en•rage

en•rich

en•roll

en•roll•ment

en•sure

en•tail

en•tan•gle

en•ter

en•tered

en•ter•prise

en•ter•pris•es

en•ter•tain

en•ter•tain•ment

en•thrall

en•thu•si•asm

en•thu•si•ast

en•thu•si•as•tic

en•tire

en•tire•ly

en•ti•tle

en•ti•tled

en•trance

en•tranc•es

en•trust

en•try

enu•mer•ate

enun•ci•ate

en•vel•op

en•ve•lope

en•ve•lopes

en•vi•ron•ment

en•vy

en•zyme

ep•ic

ep•i•lep•sy

ep•i•lep•tic

ep•i•sode

ep•och

equal

equal•i•ty

equal•ly

equate

equi•lib•ri•um

equip

equip•ment

equipped

eq•ui•ta•ble

eq•ui•ty

equiv•a•lent

era

erase

erect

erode

ero•sion

er•rand

er•ror

erupt

erup•tion

es•ca•la•tor

es•cape

es•cort

es•pe•cial

es•pe•cial•ly

es•quire

es•say

es•sen•tial

es•tab•lish

es•tab•lished

es•tab•lish•ment

es•tate

es•thet•ic

es•ti•mate

es•ti•ma•tion

eter•nal

eter•ni•ty

eth•i•cal

eth•ics

eth•nic

et•i•quette

Eur•asian

Eu•rope

Eu•ro•pe•an

eu•tha•na•sia

evac•u•ate

eval•u•ate

eval•u•a•tion

evap•o•rate

eva•sive

even

eve•ning

eve•nings

even•ly

event

event•ful

even•tu•al

even•tu•al•ly

ev•er

ev•ery

ev•ery•body

ev•ery•day

ev•ery•thing

ev•ery•where

ev•i•dence

ev•i•dent

ev•i•dent•ly

evil

evoke

evo•lu•tion

evolve

ex•act

ex•act•ly	ex•e•cute	ex•pect
ex•ag•ger•ate	ex•e•cu•tion	ex•pec•tan•cy
ex•am	ex•ec•u•tive	ex•pec•ta•tions
ex•am•ine	ex•ec•u•tor	ex•pe•dite
ex•am•ined	ex•ec•u•trix	ex•pe•di•tion
ex•am•ple	ex•em•pla•ry	ex•pe•di•tious
ex•ca•vate	ex•em•pli•fy	ex•pel
ex•ceed	ex•empt	ex•pelled
ex•ceed•ing•ly	ex•emp•tion	ex•pend
ex•cel	ex•er•cise	ex•pen•di•ture
ex•cel•lence	ex•ert	ex•pense
ex•cel•lent	ex•er•tion	ex•pens•es
ex•cept	ex•haust	ex•pen•sive
ex•cep•tion	ex•hib•it	ex•pe•ri•ence
ex•cep•tion•al	ex•hib•it•ed	ex•pe•ri•enced
ex•cess	ex•hi•bi•tion	ex•pe•ri•enc•es
ex•cess•es	ex•hil•a•rate	ex•per•i•ment
ex•ces•sive	ex•ile	ex•per•i•men•tal
ex•change	ex•ist	ex•pert
ex•cite	ex•is•tence	ex•per•tise
ex•cit•ed	ex•it	ex•pire
ex•cite•ment	ex•on•er•ate	ex•pired
ex•claim	ex•or•bi•tant	ex•plain
ex•cla•ma•tion	ex•ot•ic	ex•plained
ex•clude	ex•pand	ex•pla•na•tion
ex•cuse	ex•pand•ed	ex•plic•it
ex•cus•es	ex•pan•sion	ex•plode

ex•ploit

ex•plo•ra•tion

ex•plore

ex•plored

ex•plo•sion

ex•plo•sive

ex•po•nent

ex•port

ex•port•ed

ex•pose

ex•press

ex•pres•sion

ex•qui•site

ex•tem•po•ra•ne•ous

ex•tend

ex•ten•sion

ex•ten•sive

ex•tent

ex•ten•u•ate

ex•te•ri•or

ex•ter•mi•nate

ex•ter•nal

ex•tinct

ex•tin•guish

ex•tort

ex•tra

ex•tract

ex•tra•cur•ric•u•lar

ex•trav•a•gance

ex•trav•a•gant

ex•treme

ex•treme•ly

ex•trem•i•ty

ex•tri•cate

ex•trin•sic

ex•tro•vert

ex•u•ber•ance

ex•u•ber•ant

ex•ude

ex•ult

eye

eye•brow

eyed

eyes

eye•sight

eye•strain

eye•wit•ness

F

fa•ble

fab•ric

fab•ri•cate

fa•cade

face

faced

fac•es

fa•cil•i•tate

fa•cil•i•ties

fa•cil•i•ty

fac•sim•i•le

fact

fac•tion

fac•tor

fac•to•ry

facts

fac•tu•al

fac•ul•ties

fac•ul•ty

fade

fail

failed

fail•ure

faint

fair

fair•ly	fan•ta•sy	fau•cet
faith	far	fault
faith•ful	farce	fa•vor
fake	fare	fa•vor•able
fall	fare•well	fa•vor•ably
fal•la•cy	farm	fa•vor•ite
fall•en	farm•er	fa•vor•it•ism
fal•li•ble	far•sight•ed	fawn
fall•out	far•ther	fear
false	far•thest	fear•ful
false•hood	fas•ci•nate	fear•less
fal•si•fy	fas•ci•na•tion	fea•si•bil•i•ty
fal•ter	fash•ion	fea•si•ble
fal•tered	fash•ion•able	feast
fame	fast	feath•er
famed	fast•back	fea•ture
fa•mil•iar	fas•ten	fea•tured
fa•mil•iar•i•ty	fat	Feb•ru•ary
fam•i•lies	fa•tal	fed•er•al
fam•i•ly	fate•ful	fed•er•a•tion
fam•ine	fa•ther	fee
fa•mous	fa•ther•hood	fee•ble
fa•nat•ic	fa•ther-in-law	fee•ble•ness
fan•ci•ful	fa•ther•ly	fee•bly
fan•cy	fath•om	feed
fan•fare	fa•tigue	feed•back
fan•tas•tic	fat•ten	feed•ings

feel	fer·til·ize	fig·ure
feel·ings	fer·vent	fig·ured
fees	fer·vor	fig·u·rine
feet	fes·ter	fil·a·ment
feign	fes·ti·val	file
fe·lic·i·tate	fes·tive	filed
fel·low	fetch	fil·ings
fel·low·ship	fe·tish	fill
fel·on	feud	filled
fel·o·ny	feu·dal	fil·let
felt	fe·ver	film
fe·male	few	filmed
fem·i·nine	few·er	fil·ter
fem·i·nin·i·ty	few·est	filth
fe·mur	fi·as·co	fil·trate
fence	fi·ber	fil·tra·tion
fend	fib·u·la	fi·nal
fend·er	fick·le	fi·nal·ist
fer·ment	fic·tion	fi·nal·ly
fer·men·ta·tion	fic·tion·al	fi·nance
fern	fi·du·cia·ry	fi·nanced
fe·ro·cious	field·ed	fi·nanc·es
fe·roc·i·ty	fiend	fi·nan·cial
fer·ret	fierce	fi·nan·cial·ly
fer·ry	fi·ery	fi·nan·cier
fer·tile	fight	find
fer·til·i·ty	fig·ment	find·er

find•ings	fiz•zle	flew
fine	flag	flex
fin•est	flag•el•late	flex•i•bil•i•ty
fin•ger	fla•grance	flex•i•ble
fin•ger•print	fla•grant	flick
fin•ish	flag•ship	fli•er
fin•ished	flair	flight
fi•nite	flake	flim•sy
fir	flam•beau	flinch
fire	flam•boy•ant	fling
fired	flame	flint
fire•place	flame•proof	flirt
fire•proof	flat	float
firm	flat•ly	flock
firm•est	flaunt	flood
firm•ly	fla•vor	floor
first	flaw	flo•ral
fis•cal	flax	flo•rist
fis•sion	flea	floss
fist	fleck	floun•der
fit	fled	flour
fit•ness	fledge	flour•ish
fit•ted	flee	flout
fit•ting•ly	fleece	flow
fix	fleet	flow•er
fix•es	fleet•ing•ly	flown
fix•ture	flesh	fluc•tu•ate

fluc•tu•a•tion	fold	forc•es
flu•en•cy	fold•ed	forc•ible
flu•ent	fold•er	ford
flu•ent•ly	fo•liage	fore•arm
fluff	fo•lio	fore•cast
flu•id	folk	fore•close
flunk	fol•low	fore•clo•sure
flu•o•res•cence	fol•lowed	fore•ground
flu•o•res•cent	fol•low•er	fore•head
flu•o•ride	fond	for•eign
flu•o•ro•scope	fon•dle	fore•most
flur•ry	fond•ly	fore•run•ner
flush	fon•due	fore•see
flus•ter	font	fore•sight
flute	food	for•est
flut•ter	fool•ish	fore•ev•er
flux	foot	fore•warned
fly	foot•age	for•feit
fly•er	foot•ings	for•gave
foal	foot•note	for•get
foam	foot•wear	for•get•ful
fo•cal	for	for•give
fo•cus	for•bid	for•give•ness
fo•cused	for•bid•den	for•got
foe	force	for•got•ten
fog	forced	fork
foil	force•ful	form

for•mal	found•ry	free•think•er
for•mal•i•ty	foun•tain	freeze
for•mal•ly	fourth	freez•er
for•mat	fox	freight
formed	frac•tion	fren•zy
for•mer	frac•ture	fre•quen•cy
for•mer•ly	frag•ile	fre•quent
for•mu•la	frag•ment	fre•quent•ly
for•mu•late	frag•men•ta•tion	fresh
for•mu•lat•ed	fra•grance	fresh•en
for•mu•lates	fra•grant	fresh•man
for•mu•lat•ing	frail	fresh•men
for•mu•la•tion	frame	fret
fort	framed	fret•ful
forth	franc	fric•tion
forth•com•ing	fran•chise	Fri•day
for•tu•nate	frank	friend
for•tune	frank•ly	friend•less
fo•rum	frank•ness	friend•li•ness
for•ward	fra•ter•nal	friend•ly
for•ward•ed	fra•ter•ni•ty	friend•ship
fos•sil	fraud	friend•ships
fos•ter	fray	fright
fought	freak	fright•en
foul	free	fright•ened
found	free•dom	frig•id
foun•da•tion	free•ly	fringe

frisk	fume	fur•row
fri•vol•i•ty	fu•mi•gate	fur•ry
friv•o•lous	fun	fur•ther
from	func•tion	fur•ther•more
front	func•tion•al	fur•thest
fron•tier	func•tioned	fuse
frost	fund	fused
frost•bite	fun•da•men•tal	fu•sion
frost•ed	fund•ed	fuss
frown	fu•ner•al	fu•tile
froze	fun•gi	fu•ture
fro•zen	fun•gi•cide	
fru•gal	fun•gus	
fruit	fun•nel	
frus•trate	fun•ny	
frus•tra•tion	fur	
fry	fu•ri•ous	
fuch•sia	furl	
fu•el	fur•lough	
fu•gi•tive	fur•nace	
ful•fill	fur•nish	
ful•filled	fur•nished	
ful•fill•ment	fur•nish•es	
	fur•nish•ings	
full	fur•ni•ture	
ful•ly	fu•ror	
fum•ble	fur•ri•er	

G

gad•get	
gai•ety	
gain	
gained	
gain•ful	
ga•la	
gal•axy	
gale	
gall	
gal•lant	
gal•lery	
gal•ley	
gal•lon	
gal•lop	
ga•lore	
gam•ble	
gam•bler	
game	
gam•ut	
gang	
ga•rage	
gar•bage	
gar•den	
gar•ish	
gar•land	

gar•lic	
gar•ment	
gar•net	
gar•nish	
gar•ter	
gas	
gas•o•line	
gasp	
gas•tric	
gas•tri•tis	
gate	
gate•way	
gath•er	
gau•dy	
gauge	
gaunt•let	
gave	
gay•ly	
gaze	
ga•ze•bo	
ga•zelle	
ga•zette	
gear	
gel•a•tin	
gem	
gen•der	
gene	

ge•ne•al•o•gy	
gen•er•al•i•ty	
gen•er•al•iza•tion	
gen•er•al•ize	
gen•er•ate	
gen•er•a•tion	
ge•ner•ic	
gen•er•os•i•ty	
gen•er•ous	
gen•er•ous•ly	
gen•e•sis	
ge•nial	
ge•nius	
gen•teel	
gen•tile	
gen•tle	
gen•tle•man	
gen•tle•men	
gent•ly	
gen•u•ine	
gen•u•ine•ly	
gen•u•ine•ness	
ge•nus	
ge•ol•o•gy	
geo•met•ric	
ge•om•e•try	
ger•mi•cide	

ger•mi•nate

ger•und

ge•stalt

ges•ture

get

ghast•ly

gher•kin

ghet•to

ghost

ghoul

gi•ant

gib•let

gift

gi•gan•tic

gill

gin

gin•ger

gin•gi•vi•tis

gi•raffe

gir•dle

girl

girl•hood

gist

give

giv•en

gives

gla•cial

glad

glad•ly

glad•ness

glam•or•ous

glam•our

glance

glanced

gland

glare

glar•ing•ly

glass

glass•es

glass•ware

glau•co•ma

glaze

gleam

gleamed

glib

glide

glim•mer

glimpse

glis•ten

gloat

globe

gloom

glo•ri•fi•ca•tion

glo•ri•fy

glo•ri•ous

glo•ry

gloss

glos•sa•ry

glossy

glove

glow

glu•cose

glue

glut•ton

glyc•er•in

go

goal

goat

gob•let

god

god•child

god•dess

god•fa•ther

god•moth•er

goes

goi•ter

gold

gold•en

gold•en•rod

golf

good

good•ness

goods

good•will

goose

gor•geous

go•ril•la

gos•sip

got

Goth•ic

got•ten

gour•met

gov•ern

gov•erned

gov•ern•ment

gov•er•nor

gov•erns

gown

grab

grace

grace•ful

gra•cious

grade

grad•ed

grad•u•al

grad•u•al•ly

grad•u•ate

grad•u•at•ed

grad•u•a•tion

graf•fi•ti

grain

gram•mar

gram•mat•i•cal

grand

grand•child

gran•deur

grand•fa•ther

grand•moth•er

grand•par•ent

grand•son

gran•ite

grant

grant•ed

gran•u•lar

gran•u•lat•ed

gran•ule

grape

graph

graph•ic

grasp

grass

grate

grate•ful

grate•ful•ly

grat•i•fi•ca•tion

grat•i•tude

gra•tu•ity

grav•i•tate

grav•i•ty

gra•vy

gray

graze

grease

great

great•est

great•ly

great•ness

greed

greed•i•ly

Greek

green•house

greet

greet•ings

grew

grief

grieve

griev•ous

grill

gri•mace

grin

grind

grip

gripe	guid•ance	**H**
groan	guide	hab•it
gro•cer	guide•book	hab•i•tat
gro•cery	guid•ed	ha•bit•u•al
groin	guide•line	had
groom	guild	had•dock
groove	guile	hadn't
gross	guil•lo•tine	hag•gard
gro•tesque	guilt	hail
ground	guin•ea	hair
group	gui•tar	hair•brush
group•ings	gulf	hair•cut
grove	gull•ible	half
grow	gum	half•tone
growl	gun	hal•i•but
grown	gust	hal•i•to•sis
growth	gut•ter	hal•lu•ci•na•tion
grudge	guy	ha•lo
gruff	gym	halt
guar•an•tee	gym•na•si•um	halves
guar•an•tees	gym•nast	ham
guar•an•ty	gym•nas•tic	ham•mer
guard•ian	gy•ne•col•o•gist	ham•per
guards		hand
guess	gy•ne•col•o•gy	hand•bill
guessed		hand•book
guest		

hand•ful	hard•est	Ha•wai•ian
hand•i•cap	hard•ly	hawk
hand•i•capped	hard•ship	hay
han•dle	hard•ware	haz•ard
han•dled	hark	haz•ard•ous
hand•some	harm	haze
hand•writ•ten	harmed	ha•zel
handy	harm•ful	hazy
hang	harm•less	he
hanged	har•mo•ni•ous	head
hang•ings	har•mo•nize	head•ache
hang•up	har•mo•ny	head•ed
hap•haz•ard	har•ness	head•gear
hap•pen	harp	head•ings
hap•pened	harsh	head•light
hap•pen•ings	har•vest	head•line
hap•pi•er	has	head•phone
hap•pi•est	haste	head•quar•ters
hap•pi•ly	has•ten	head•stone
hap•pi•ness	hast•i•ly	head•way
hap•py	hat	heal
ha•rass	hate	healed
ha•rass•ment	hate•ful	health
har•bor	ha•tred	health•ful
hard	haugh•ty	healthy
hard•en	haul	heap
hard•er	haunt	hear

heard

hear•ings

hear•say

heart

heart•ache

heart•beat

heart•break

hearth

hearty

heat

heat•ed

heat•er

hea•then

heath•er

heav•en

heavi•ly

heavy

heck•le

hec•tic

hedge

heed

heed•ed

heed•less

heel

height

height•en

height•ened

heir

heir•ess

held

he•li•cop•ter

he•li•um

helm

hel•met

help

helped

help•ful

help•ful•ly

help•ful•ness

help•less

help•less•ly

hem

hemi•sphere

hem•lock

hem•or•rhage

hemp

hence

hence•forth

hence•for•ward

hep•a•ti•tis

her

her•ald

herb

herb•al

herd

herd•ed

here

here•abouts

here•af•ter

here•by

he•red•i•tary

he•red•i•ty

here•in•af•ter

her•e•sy

here•to

here•to•fore

here•un•to

here•with

her•i•tage

her•nia

he•ro

he•ro•ic

her•o•ine

her•pes

her•self

hes•i•tance

hes•i•tant

hes•i•tate

hes•i•ta•tion

het•er•o•ge•neous

hexa•gon

hi•ber•nate	his•to•ry	hon•es•ty
hi•bis•cus	hit	hon•ey
hid	hoarse	hon•or
hid•den	hoax	hon•or•able
hide	hob•by	hon•or•ably
hi•er•ar•chy	hoe	hon•o•rar•i•um
high	hog	hon•or•ary
high•er	hoist	hon•ored
high•est	hold	hood
high•land	hold•ings	hook
high•ly	hole	hook•worm
high•way	hol•i•day	hope
hi•jack	hol•low	hoped
hi•lar•i•ous	ho•lo•caust	hope•ful
hill	ho•ly	hope•ful•ly
him	home	hope•less
him•self	home•like	hope•less•ly
hind	homes	hopes
hin•der	home•ward	horde
hin•drance	home•work	ho•ri•zon
hint	ho•mi•cide	hor•i•zon•tal
hip•po•drome	ho•mo•ge•ne•ity	hor•mone
hip•po•pot•a•mus	ho•mo•ge•neous	horn
hire	ho•mog•e•nize	hor•net
hired	hom•onym	horo•scope
his	hon•est	hor•ri•ble
his•tor•i•cal	hon•est•ly	hor•ri•fy

hor•ror

horse

horse•back

horse•pow•er

hose

hos•pi•tal

hos•pi•tal•i•ty

hos•pi•tal•iza•tion

hos•pi•tal•ize

host

hos•tage

host•ess

hos•tile

hos•til•i•ty

hot

ho•tel

hound

hour

hour•ly

hours

house

house•hold

house•keep•er

hous•es

house•wife

house•work

hov•er

how

howl

how•so•ev•er

hud•dle

hue

hug

huge

hulk

hu•man

hu•mane

hu•man•is•tic

hu•man•i•tar•i•an

hu•man•i•ty

hu•man•kind

hu•man•ly

hum•ble

hu•mid

hu•mid•i•fi•er

hu•mid•i•fy

hu•mid•i•ty

hu•mil•i•ate

hu•mil•i•a•tion

hu•mil•i•ty

hu•mor

hu•mor•ist

hu•mor•ous

hump

hu•mus

hunch

hun•dred

hung

hun•ger

hun•gry

hunt

hunt•er

hur•dle

hurl

hurled

hur•ri•cane

hur•ried

hur•ry

hurt

hurt•ful

hus•band

hush

husk

hus•ky

hus•tle

hy•brid

hy•drant

hy•drau•lic

hy•dro•car•bon

hy•dro•gen

hy•dro•pho•bia

hy•giene

hy•gien•ic

hy•per•bo•le

hy•phen

hy•phen•ate

hyp•no•sis

hyp•not•ic

hyp•no•tist

hyp•no•tize

hy•po•chon•dria

hy•po•chon•dri•ac

hy•poc•ri•sy

hyp•o•crite

hy•po•der•mic

hy•poth•e•ses

hy•poth•e•sis

hy•po•thet•i•cal

hys•te•ria

hys•ter•i•cal

I

Ibe•ri•an

ice

ice•berg

ici•cle

idea

ide•al

ide•al•ist

ide•al•is•tic

ide•al•ly

ide•as

iden•ti•cal

iden•ti•fi•ca•tion

iden•ti•fi•ca•tions

iden•ti•fy

iden•ti•ty

ide•ol•o•gy

id•i•om

id•io•syn•cra•sy

id•io•syn•crat•ic

id•i•ot

idle

idol

idol•ize

idyl•lic

if

ig•nite

ig•ni•tion

ig•no•rance

ig•no•rant

ig•nore

ig•nored

ill

il•le•gal

il•le•gal•i•ty

il•le•git•i•ma•cy

il•le•git•i•mate

il•lic•it

il•lit•er•ate

ill•ness

il•log•i•cal

il•lu•mi•nate

il•lu•mi•na•tion

il•lu•sion

il•lu•sive

il•lus•trate

il•lus•tra•tion

il•lus•tri•ous

im•age

im•ag•ery

imag•i•na•tion

imag•ine

imag•ined

im•be•cile

im•i•tate

im•i•ta•tion

im•mac•u•late

im•ma•te•ri•al

im•ma•ture

im•ma•tu•rity

im•me•di•ate

im•me•di•ate•ly

im•mense

im•mense•ly

im•merse

im•mersed

im•mer•sion

im•mi•grant

im•mi•grate

im•mi•gra•tion

im•mi•nence

im•mi•nent

im•mo•bil•i•ty

im•mo•bi•lize

im•mod•est

im•mor•al

im•mor•tal

im•mov•able

im•mune

im•mu•ni•ty

im•mu•nize

im•pact

im•pair

im•part

im•par•tial

im•par•tial•i•ty

im•par•tial•ly

im•passe

im•pas•sion

im•pas•sive

im•pa•tience

im•pa•tient

im•peach

im•peach•ment

im•pec•ca•bil•i•ty

im•pec•ca•ble

im•pede

im•ped•i•ment

im•per•a•tive

im•per•fect

im•per•fec•tion

im•pe•ri•al

im•pe•ri•al•ist

im•per•son•al

im•per•son•ate

im•pet•u•ous

im•pe•tus

im•pinge

imp•ish

im•plant

im•plau•si•ble

im•ple•ment

im•ple•ment•ed

im•pli•cate

im•pli•ca•tion

im•plic•it

im•plore

im•ply

im•po•lite

im•port

im•por•tance

im•por•tant

im•por•tant•ly

im•port•ed

im•pose

im•pos•si•bil•i•ty

im•pos•si•ble

im•po•tence

im•po•tent

im•pov•er•ish

im•preg•na•ble

im•preg•nate

im•press

im•pres•sion

im•pres•sion•able

im•pres•sive

im•print

im•pris•on

im•prob•a•bil•i•ty

im•prob•a•ble

im•promp•tu

im•prop•er

im•pro•pri•ety

im•prov•able

im•prove

im•prove•ment

im•pro•vi•sa•tion

im•pro•vise

im•pulse

im•pul•sive

im•pure

im•pu•ri•ty

in

in•abil•i•ty

in•ac•ces•si•ble

in•ac•cu•ra•cy

in•ac•cu•rate

in•ac•tion

in•ac•tive

in•ad•e•quate

in•alien•able

in•an•i•mate

in•ap•pro•pri•ate

in•as•much

in•au•di•ble

in•au•di•bly

in•au•gu•ral

in•au•gu•rate

in•au•gu•ra•tion

in•born

in•bred

in•can•des•cence

in•ca•pa•ble

in•ca•pac•i•tate

in•ca•pac•i•ty

in•car•nate

in•car•na•tion

in•cen•tive

in•cep•tion

in•ces•sant

in•cest

inch

inch•es

in•ci•dence

in•ci•dent

in•ci•den•tal

in•cin•er•ate

in•cise

in•ci•sion

in•ci•sor

in•cite

in•clem•ent

in•cline

in•clined

in•clude

in•clud•ed

in•clu•sion

in•clu•sive

in•co•her•ence

in•co•her•ent

in•come

in•com•pa•ra•ble

in•com•pa•ra•bly

in•com•pat•i•bil•i•ty

in•com•pat•i•ble

in•com•pe•tence

in•com•pe•tent

in•com•plete

in•com•pre•hen•si•ble

in•con•sid•er•ate

in•con•sis•tent

in•con•spic•u•ous

in•con•ve•nience

in•con•ve•nienced

in•con•ve•nient

in•con•ve•nient•ly

in•cor•po•rate

in•cor•po•rat•ed

in•cor•rect

in•crease

in•creased

in•creas•es

in•cred•ibil•i•ty

in•cred•i•ble

in•cre•ment

in•crim•i•nate

in•cum•bent

in•cur

in•curred

in•debt•ed

in•de•cen•cy

in•de•cent

in•deed

in•def•i•nite

in•dem•ni•ty

in•dent

in•den•tion

in•de•pen•dence

in•de•pen•dent

in•dex

in•dexed

in•dex•es

in•di•cate

in•di•ca•tion

in•dic•a•tive

in•dict

in•dict•ed

in•dict•ment

in•dif•fer•ence

in•dif•fer•ent

in•dif•fer•ent•ly

in•dig•e•nous

in•dig•ni•ty

in•di•rect

in•di•rect•ly

in•dis•creet

in•dis•cre•tion

in•dis•pens•able

in•dite

in•di•vid•u•al

in•di•vid•u•al•i•ty

in•di•vid•u•al•ize

in•di•vid•u•al•ly

in•di•vis•i•ble

in•doc•tri•nate

in•duce

in•duct

in•duc•tion

in•dulge

in•dul•gence

in•dul•gent

in•dus•tri•al

in•dus•tries

in•dus•tri•ous

in•dus•try

in•elas•tic

in•el•i•gi•ble

in•ept

in•eq•ui•ty

in•er•tia

in•ex•pen•sive

in•ex•pe•ri•ence

in•fant

in•fan•tile

in•fat•u•ate

in•fect

in•fec•tion

in•fer

in•fer•ence

in•fer•en•tial

in•fe•ri•or

in•fe•ri•or•i•ty

in•fer•tile	in•fuse	ink
in•fest	in•ge•nious	inked
in•fi•del•i•ty	in•ge•nu•ity	in•land
in•fil•trate	in•grate	inn
in•fi•nite	in•gra•ti•ate	in•nate
in•fin•i•ty	in•gre•di•ent	in•ner
in•flame	in•hab•it•ant	in•no•cence
in•flam•ma•tion	in•hale	in•no•cent
in•flam•ma•to•ry	in•her•ent	in•no•cent•ly
in•fla•tion	in•her•it	in•noc•u•ous
in•fla•tion•ary	in•her•i•tance	in•no•vate
in•flect	in•hib•it	in•no•va•tion
in•flict	in•hu•mane	in•nu•en•do
in•flu•ence	in•im•i•cal	in•nu•mer•a•ble
in•flu•en•tial	ini•tial	in•oc•u•late
in•flu•en•za	ini•tialed	in•op•er•a•ble
in•form	ini•tial•ly	in•or•gan•ic
in•for•mal	ini•tials	in•put
in•for•mal•i•ty	ini•ti•ate	in•quest
in•for•mal•ly	ini•ti•a•tion	in•quire
in•for•ma•tion	in•ject	in•quired
in•for•ma•tion•al	in•jec•tion	in•quires
in•formed	in•junc•tion	in•qui•ries
in•frac•tion	in•jure	in•qui•ry
in•fre•quent•ly	in•ju•ries	in•qui•si•tion
in•fringe	in•ju•ry	in•sane
in•fu•ri•ate	in•jus•tice	in•san•i•ty

in•sa•tia•ble

in•scribe

in•scrip•tion

in•sect

in•sec•ti•cide

in•se•cure

in•se•cu•ri•ty

in•sep•a•ra•ble

in•sert

in•ser•tion

in•set

in•side

in•sight

in•sig•nif•i•cance

in•sig•nif•i•cant

in•sin•cere

in•sin•u•ate

in•sist

in•sis•tence

in•sis•tent

in•som•nia

in•som•ni•ac

in•so•much

in•spect

in•spec•tion

in•spi•ra•tion

in•spi•ra•tion•al

in•spire

in•sta•bil•i•ty

in•stall

in•stal•la•tion

in•stall•ment

in•stance

in•stanc•es

in•stant

in•stant•ly

in•stead

in•sti•gate

in•still

in•stinct

in•stinc•tive

in•sti•tute

in•sti•tut•ed

in•sti•tu•tion

in•struct

in•struc•tion

in•struc•tor

in•stru•ment

in•sub•or•di•nate

in•suf•fi•cient

in•su•late

in•su•lat•ed

in•su•la•tion

in•su•lin

in•sult

in•sult•ed

in•sur•abil•i•ty

in•sur•able

in•sur•ance

in•sure

in•sured

in•sures

in•tact

in•take

in•te•gral

in•te•grate

in•teg•ri•ty

in•tel•lect

in•tel•lec•tu•al

in•tel•li•gence

in•tel•li•gent

in•tel•li•gi•ble

in•tend

in•tend•ed

in•tense

in•ten•si•fy

in•ten•si•ty

in•tent

in•ten•tion

in•ten•tion•al•ly

in•tent•ly

in•ter•act

in•ter•ac•tion

in•ter•cede

in•ter•cept

in•ter•cep•tion

in•ter•change

in•ter•com

in•ter•de•pen•dence

in•ter•de•pen•dent

in•ter•est

in•ter•est•ed

in•ter•est•ing•ly

in•ter•face

in•ter•fere

in•ter•fered

in•ter•fer•ence

in•ter•im

in•te•ri•or

in•ter•ject

in•ter•me•di•ate

in•ter•mis•sion

in•ter•mit•tent

in•tern

in•ter•nal

in•ter•na•tion•al

in•ter•pret

in•ter•pre•ta•tion

in•ter•ro•gate

in•ter•rupt

in•ter•rup•tion

in•ter•sect

in•ter•state

in•ter•val

in•ter•vene

in•ter•view

in•ter•viewed

in•tes•tate

in•tes•tine

in•ti•ma•cy

in•ti•mate

in•tim•i•date

in•tim•i•da•tion

in•to

in•tol•er•a•ble

in•tox•i•cate

in•tra•ve•nous

in•tri•ca•cy

in•tri•cate

in•trigue

in•trin•sic

in•tro•duce

in•tro•duced

in•tro•duc•es

in•tro•duc•tion

in•tro•spect

in•tro•vert

in•trude

in•tu•ition

in•tu•itive

in•vade

in•val•id

in•val•i•date

in•vent

in•ven•tion

in•ven•to•ry

in•vest

in•ves•ti•gate

in•vest•ment

in•ves•tor

in•vig•o•rate

in•vis•i•bly

in•vi•ta•tion

in•vi•ta•tion•al

in•vite

in•voice

in•voic•es

in•voke

in•vol•un•tary

in•volve

in•ward

in•ward•ly

J

Ira•ni•an	jack•et	jour•nal•ism
irate	jade	jour•nal•ist
Irish	jail	jour•ney
iron	jan•i•tor	joy
iron•ic	Jan•u•ary	joy•ful
ir•ra•tio•nal	Jap•a•nese	joy•ful•ly
ir•reg•u•lar	jar	joy•ous
ir•reg•u•lar•i•ty	jeal•ous	judge
ir•rel•e•vant	jeal•ou•sy	judged
ir•ri•gate	jeop•ar•dy	judg•ment
ir•ri•tate	jet	ju•di•cial
is	jet•lin•er	ju•di•cia•ry
Is•lam	jew•el•er	juice
is•land	jew•el•ry	Ju•ly
isle	Jew•ry	jump
isn't	jinx	junc•tion
iso•late	job	June
iso•la•tion	join	ju•nior
is•su•ance	joined	juries
is•sue	joint	ju•ris•dic•tion
is•sues	joint•ly	ju•ror
ital•ic	joke	ju•ry
item	jol•ly	just
item•ize	jolt	jus•ti•fi•ca•tion
its	jour•nal	jus•ti•fy
it•self		just•ly
		ju•ve•nile

K

keen

keep

keep•sake

kept

key•board

key•note

kid•nap

kid•ney

kill

kind

kind•ly

kind•ness

king•dom

kiss

kit

kitch•en

kite

knee

knee•cap

kneel

knelt

knew

knife

knit

knot

know

know•ing•ly

knowl•edge

known

knows

Ko•dak

Ko•ran

Ko•re•an

kosh•er

L

la•bel

la•beled

la•bor

lab•o•ra•to•ry

la•bored

la•bor•er

lace

lac•er•ate

lack

lad•der

la•dies

la•dy

lake

lame

la•ment

lam•i•nate

lamp

land

land•ed

land•own•er

lan•guage

lan•o•lin

lapse

lapsed

lar•ce•ny

large	la•zi•ness	le•gal•ize
larg•er	la•zy	le•gal•ly
larg•est	lead	leg•end
lar•yn•gi•tis	lead•er	leg•i•ble
lar•ynx	lead•er•ship	leg•is•late
lass	leaf	leg•is•la•ture
last	leaf•let	
last•ing•ly	leaf•lets	
late	league	le•git•i•mate
late•ly	leak	lei•sure
lat•er	lean	lem•on
lat•er•al	leap	lend
lat•est	learn	length
lath•er	learned	length•en
lat•i•tude	lease	lengthy
lat•ter	leased	le•nien•cy
laugh	leash	le•nient
laugh•ter	least	lens
launch	leath•er	less
laun•dry	leave	les•see
law	lec•ture	less•en
law•ful	lec•tured	less•ened
lawn	led	les•son
law•suit	led•ger	let
law•yer	left	le•thar•gic
lay	leg•a•cy	let•ter
lay•er	le•gal	let•ter•head
		let•tuce

leu•ke•mia	lift•ed	liq•uid
lev•el	lig•a•ment	liq•ui•date
le•ver	light	list
le•ver•age	light•en	list•ed
li•a•bil•i•ties	light•ly	lis•ten
li•a•bil•i•ty	light•ning	lis•tened
li•a•ble	lik•able	lis•ten•er
li•ai•son	like	list•ings
li•ar	liked	lit•er•a•cy
li•bel	like•li•hood	lit•er•al
lib•er•al	like•ly	lit•er•a•ture
lib•er•ate	limb	lit•i•gate
lib•er•ty	lim•it	lit•i•ga•tion
li•brar•i•an	lim•i•ta•tion	lit•tle
li•brar•ies	lim•it•ed	live
li•brary	lim•ou•sine	lived
li•cense	line	live•li•hood
li•censed	lined	load
li•cens•es	lin•en	loan
lie	lin•ger	loaned
lien	lin•ge•rie	loans
liens	lin•guist	lob•by
lieu	lin•ing	lob•ster
lieu•ten•ant	lin•ings	lo•cal
life	link	lo•cal•i•ty
life•time	li•on	lo•cate
lift	liq•ue•fy	lo•cat•ed

lo•ca•tion

lo•ca•tions

lock

locked

lock•out

lo•co•mo•tive

lodge

lodg•ings

log•ic

log•i•cal

log•i•cal•ly

loi•ter

lone•ly

long

long•er

long•est

lon•gev•i•ty

long•hand

long•ings

lon•gi•tude

look

looked

look•out

looks

loose

loose•ly

loos•en

lord

lose

los•er

los•es

loss

loss•es

lost

lot

lo•tion

lot•tery

loud

loud•ly

lounge

lov•able

love

love•ly

lov•ing•ly

low

low•est

loy•al

loy•al•ly

loy•al•ty

lu•bri•cate

lu•cid

luck

lucky

lug•gage

lum•ber

lu•mi•nous

lunch

lun•cheon

lung

lungs

lu•rid

Lu•ther•an

M

mac•a•ro•ni

mac•a•roon

ma•chine

ma•chin•ery

ma•chines

mad

made

mag•a•zine

mag•a•zines

mag•ic

mag•i•cal

mag•net

mag•net•ic

mag•nif•i•cent

mag•ni•fy

maid

mail

mail•able

mailed

main

main•ly

main•tain

main•tained

main•tains

main•te•nance

ma•jor

ma•jor•i•ties

ma•jor•i•ty

make

mal•ad•just•ed

mal•ad•just•ment

male

mal•fea•sance

mal•ice

ma•li•cious

ma•lign

ma•lig•nant

mall

mal•prac•tice

mam•mal

mam•ma•ry

man

man•age

man•aged

man•age•ment

man•ag•er

man•ag•es

man•date

ma•neu•ver

man•hood

ma•ni•ac

man•i•fest

ma•nip•u•late

ma•nip•u•lat•ed

ma•nip•u•la•tion

man•ly

man•ner

man•sion

man•u•al

man•u•al•ly

man•u•als

man•u•fac•ture

man•u•fac•tured

man•u•fac•tur•er

man•u•fac•tures

manu•script

many

map

March

mar•ga•rine

mar•gin

mar•i•jua•na

ma•rine

mar•i•tal

mark

marked

mar•ket

mar•ket•abil•i•ty

mar•ket•able

mar•ket•place	may•or	meet
mar•riage	me	meet•ings
Mars	mea•ger	mel•o•dy
mass•es	mean	mem•ber
mas•ter	mean•ing•ful	mem•ber•ships
mas•tered	meant	mem•brane
mas•tery	mean•time	me•men•to
match	mean•while	mem•oir
ma•te•ri•al	mea•sur•able	mem•o•ra•ble
ma•te•ri•al•ize	mea•sure	mem•o•ran•da
math	mea•sure•ment	mem•o•ran•dum
math•e•mat•i•cal	me•chan•ic	me•mo•ri•al
ma•tri•arch	me•chan•i•cal	mem•o•rize
mat•ri•mo•ny	med•al	mem•o•ry
ma•trix	me•dia	mend
mat•ter	me•di•an	mend•ed
mat•tress	me•di•ate	men•tal
ma•ture	me•di•a•tion	men•tion
ma•tured	med•i•cal	men•tioned
ma•tures	medi•care	men•tor
ma•tu•ri•ty	med•i•cate	menu
max•i•mize	med•i•cine	mer•can•tile
max•i•mum	me•di•o•cre	mer•ce•nary
may	med•i•tate	mer•chan•dise
May	me•di•um	mer•chant
may•be	me•dul•la	mere•ly
	meek	merge

merged

merg•er

mer•it

mes•sage

mes•sag•es

mes•sen•ger

met

met•al

me•ter

meth•od

me•thod•i•cal

me•tic•u•lous

met•ric

met•ro•pol•i•tan

Mex•i•can

mi•cro•chip

mi•cro•fiche

mi•cro•film

mi•cro•phone

mi•cro•scope

mid•dle

mid•dle•man

midg•et

mid•night

midst

might

might•i•ly

mi•grate

mild

mild•ly

mile

mile•age

mil•i•tary

milk

mill

mil•lion

mind

mind•ful

mine

min•er•al

min•ia•ture

min•i•mal

min•i•mize

min•i•mum

min•is•ter

mi•nor

mi•nor•i•ties

mi•nor•i•ty

mi•nus

min•ute

mir•a•cle

mir•ror

mis•be•hav•ior

mis•cal•cu•late

mis•car•riage

mis•cel•la•neous

mis•chief

mis•chie•vous

mis•con•cep•tion

mis•con•strue

mis•de•mean•or

mis•di•rect

mis•ery

mis•for•tune

mis•giv•ings

mis•hap

mis•in•form

mis•in•formed

mis•in•ter•pret

mis•in•ter•pre•ta•tion

mis•in•ter•pret•ed

mis•judge

mis•judged

mis•laid

mis•lead

mis•led

mis•place

mis•placed

mis•plac•es

mis•print

mis•quote

mis•rep•re•sent

mis•rep•re•sen•ta•tion

miss

Miss

missed

mis•sile

mis•sion

mis•spell

mis•state

mis•take

mis•tak•en

mis•tak•en•ly

mis•takes

mis•trust

mis•un•der•stand

mis•un•der•stand•ings

mis•un•der•stood

mis•use

mix

mixed

mix•ture

mo•bile

mo•bil•i•ty

mo•bi•lize

mode

mod•el

mod•er•ate

mod•er•a•tion

mod•ern

mod•ern•ize

mod•est

mod•i•fi•ca•tion

mod•i•fy

moist

mois•ture

mold

mom

mo•ment

mo•men•tari•ly

mo•men•tum

mon•ar•chy

Mon•day

mon•e•tary

mon•ey

mon•ies

mon•i•tor

mo•nog•a•mous

mo•nog•a•my

mono•gram

mono•graph

mo•nop•o•lize

mo•nop•o•ly

mo•not•o•nous

mo•not•o•ny

month

month•ly

mon•u•ment

mood

moon

moot

more

more•over

morn•ing

morn•ings

mort•gage

mort•gaged

mor•ti•fy

Mos•lem

most

mo•tel

mo•tion

mo•tioned

mo•tions

mo•ti•vate

mo•ti•vat•ed

mo•ti•va•tion

mo•tive

mo•tor

mo•tor•cy•cle

mo•tor•ist

mot•to

mount

moun•tain

mourn

mouth

mov•able

move

move•ment

Mr.

Mrs.

Ms.

much

muf•fin

mul•ti•ple

mul•ti•ply

mun•dane

mu•nic•i•pal

mu•ral

mur•der

mur•mur

mus•cle

mush•room

mu•sic

mu•si•cal

mu•si•cian

must

mu•ti•late

mu•tu•al

mu•tu•al•ly

my

my•self

mys•te•ri•ous

mys•tery

mys•tic

mys•ti•cal

mys•ti•fy

myth

my•thol•o•gy

N

nail

na•ive

na•ive•té

name

named

name•ly

nap•kin

nar•rate

nar•ra•tion

nar•ra•tive

nar•ra•tor

nar•row

nar•row•ly

na•sal

nas•ty

na•tion

na•tion•al

na•tion•al•ly

na•tions

na•tion•wide

na•tive

nat•u•ral

nat•u•ral•ly

na•ture

nau•sea

nau•seous

na•val

nav•i•gate

na•vy

near

near•by

near•ly

neat

neat•ly

nec•es•sar•i•ly

nec•es•sary

ne•ces•si•tate

ne•ces•si•tat•ed

ne•ces•si•ty

need

need•ed

nee•dle

need•less

need•less•ly

ne•gate

neg•a•tive

ne•glect

neg•li•gence

neg•li•gent

ne•go•tia•ble

ne•go•ti•ate

ne•go•ti•a•tion

ne•go•ti•a•tor

neigh•bor

neigh•bor•hood

neigh•bor•ly

nei•ther

neph•ew

nerve

ner•vous

net

net•work

neu•ro•sis

neu•rot•ic

neu•tral

neu•tral•ize

nev•er

nev•er•the•less

new

news

news•casts

news•let•ter

news•pa•per

news•pa•pers

next

nice

nice•ly

niece

night

night•ly

ni•tro•gen

no

no•bil•i•ty

no•body

noise

noisy

nom•i•nal

nom•i•nate

nom•i•nat•ed

nom•i•na•tion

nom•i•nee

non•cha•lant

non•es•sen•tial

non•res•i•dent

non•sense

non•stop

noon

nor

norm

nor•mal

north

north•east

north•east•ern

north•ern

north•ward

north•west

nose

not

no•ta•ble

no•ta•ry

no•ta•tion

note

note•book

not•ed

note•wor•thy

noth•ing

no•tice

no•tice•able

no•ticed

no•tic•es

no•ti•fi•ca•tion

no•ti•fi•ca•tions

no•ti•fied

no•ti•fies

no•ti•fy

no•tion

no•to•ri•ety

no•to•ri•ous

not•with•stand•ing

noun

nour•ish

nour•ished

nov•el

No•vem•ber

nov•ice

now

no•where

nu•cle•ar

nui•sance

num•ber

num•bered

num•bers

nu•mer•ic

nu•mer•ous

nurse

nur•ture

nu•tri•ent

nu•tri•tion

nu•tri•tious

ny•lon

O

oath

obe•di•ent

obey

ob•ject

ob•ject•ed

ob•jec•tion

ob•jec•tion•able

ob•jec•tions

ob•jec•tive

ob•jec•tives

ob•jec•tiv•i•ty

ob•jects

ob•li•gate

ob•li•gat•ed

ob•li•ga•tion

oblige

obliv•i•ous

ob•long

ob•nox•ious

ob•scene

ob•scure

ob•ser•vant

ob•ser•va•tion

ob•serve

ob•sess

ob•sessed

ob•ses•sion

ob•so•les•cence

ob•so•les•cent

ob•so•lete

ob•sta•cle

ob•stet•rics

ob•sti•nate

ob•struct

ob•struct•ed

ob•tain

ob•tain•able

ob•vi•ous

ob•vi•ous•ly

oc•ca•sion

oc•ca•sion•al

oc•ca•sion•al•ly

oc•ca•sions

oc•cu•pan•cy

oc•cu•pant

oc•cu•pa•tion

oc•cu•pa•tions

oc•cu•pied

oc•cu•pies

oc•cu•py

oc•cur

oc•curred

oc•cur•rence

oc•curs

ocean

Oc•to•ber

odd

odor

of

off

of•fend

of•fense

of•fen•sive

of•fer

of•fered

of•fer•ings

of•fice

of•fi•cer

of•fi•cers

of•fic•es

of•fi•cial

of•fi•cial•ly

of•fi•cials

of•fi•ci•ate

off•set

of•ten

oil

old

old•est

old-fash•ioned

om•i•nous

omis•sion

omit

omit•ted

on

once

one

one•self

on•ly

on•set

on•to

on•ward

open

opened

open•ings

open•ness

op•er•a•ble

op•er•ate

op•er•at•ed

op•er•a•tion

op•er•a•tion•al

op•er•a•tions

op•er•a•tor

opin•ion

opin•ion•at•ed

opin•ions

op•po•nent	or•di•nance	our
op•por•tune	or•di•nari•ly	ours
op•por•tu•ni•ty	or•di•nary	our•self
op•pose	or•gan	our•selves
op•posed	or•gan•ic	out
op•pos•es	or•ga•ni•za•tion	out•come
op•po•site	or•ga•ni•za•tion•al	out•door
op•po•si•tion	or•ga•ni•za•tions	out•growth
op•press	or•ga•nize	out•let
opt	or•ga•nized	out•line
opt•ed	or•ga•niz•es	out•lined
op•tic	ori•ent	out•live
op•ti•mism	or•i•gin	out•look
op•ti•mis•tic	orig•i•nal	out•ly•ing
op•ti•mum	orig•i•nal•ly	out•mod•ed
op•tion	orig•i•nate	out•put
op•tion•al	orig•i•nat•ed	out•ra•geous
op•tom•e•trist	orig•i•na•tion	out•ward•ly
or	or•phan	ova•tion
oral	os•cil•late	over
oral•ly	os•ten•si•ble	over•book
or•a•tor	os•ten•si•bly	over•charge
or•ches•tra	oth•er	over•come
or•deal	oth•ers	over•do
or•der	oth•er•wise	over•done
or•dered	ought	over•draw
or•der•ly	ounce	over•drawn

over•due

over•es•ti•mate

over•flow

over•head

over•heat

over•look

over•looked

over•ly

over•night

over•paid

over•pay

over•pay•ment

over•qual•i•fied

over•rate

over•see

over•sight

over•state

over•turn

over•turned

over•work

over•worked

owe

owed

own

owned

own•er

own•er•ship

P

pac•i•fy

pack

pack•age

pack•aged

pack•ag•es

pag•es

paid

pain

pain•ful

pain•less

paint

paint•ings

pair

pam•per

pam•phlet

pan•cre•as

pan•el

pan•eled

pan•ic

pan•icked

pan•ora•ma

pa•per

par

par•a•dox

para•graph

para•graphs

parallel

pa•ral•y•sis

par•a•lyze

para•med•ic

par•a•mount

para•noia

para•noid

para•phrase

para•ple•gic

para•pro•fes•sion•al

par•a•site

par•cel

par•don

par•ent

par•ent•hood

parked

park•way

pa•role

part

part•ed

par•tic•i•pant

par•tic•i•pants

par•tic•i•pate

par•tic•i•pat•ed

par•tic•i•pa•tion

par•ti•cle

par•ti•cles

par•tic•u•lar

par•tic•u•lar•ly

part•ly

part•ners

part•ner•ship

parts

par•ty

pass

pas•sage

pass•book

passed

pas•sen•ger

pass•es

pas•sion

pas•sive

pass•port

past

pas•time

pat•ent

pat•ent•ed

pa•ter•nal

path

pa•tience

pa•tient

pa•tient•ly

pa•tients

pa•tri•arch

pa•tri•ot

pa•tri•ot•ic

pa•tri•o•tism

pa•trol

pa•tron

pa•tron•age

pa•tron•ize

pat•tern

pause

pave

paved

pave•ment

pay

pay•able

pay•check

pay•day

pay•ee

pay•er

pay•ment

pay•ments

pay•roll

peace

peace•ful

peak

pearl

pe•cu•liar

ped•a•go•gy

pe•dan•tic

pe•des•tri•an

peer

pel•vic

pel•vis

pen

pe•nal•ize

pen•al•ties

pen•al•ty

pen•cil

pend

pen•e•trate

pen•i•cil•lin

pen•in•su•la

pen•nies

pen•ny

pen•sion

pen•sive

peo•ple

per•ceive

per•cent

per•cent•age

per•cep•tion

per•cep•tive

pe•ren•ni•al

per•fect

per•fect•ed

per•fec•tion

per•fect•ly

per•fo•rate

per•fo•rat•ed

per•fo•ra•tion

per•form

per•for•mance

per•formed

per•form•er

pe•ri•od

pe•ri•od•ic

pe•ri•od•i•cal

pe•ri•od•i•cal•ly

pe•ri•od•i•cals

pe•ri•ods

per•ish

per•ish•able

per•ished

per•jure

per•jured

per•ju•ry

per•ma•nence

per•ma•nent

per•ma•nent•ly

per•me•ate

per•mis•si•ble

per•mis•sion

per•mit

per•mit•ted

per•pe•trate

per•pet•u•al

per•pet•u•ate

per•plex

per•plexed

per•plex•ing•ly

per•se•cute

per•se•ver•ance

per•se•vere

per•sist

per•sist•ed

per•sis•tence

per•sis•tent

per•son

per•son•able

per•son•al

per•son•al•i•ties

per•son•al•i•ty

per•son•al•ly

per•son•nel

per•spec•tive

per•spi•ra•tion

per•spire

per•suade

per•suad•ed

per•sua•sion

per•sua•sive

per•tain

per•tained

per•ti•na•cious

per•ti•nent

per•turb

per•turbed

pe•rus•al

pe•ruse

pes•si•mism

pes•si•mist

pes•si•mis•tic

pet

pe•tite

pe•ti•tion

pe•tro•leum

pet•ti•ness

pet•ty

pet•u•lant

phar•ma•ceu•ti•cal

phar•ma•cist

phar•ma•cy

phase

phe•nom•e•na

phe•nom•e•non

phi•lan•thro•py

philo•soph•i•cal

phi•los•o•phy

pho•bia

phone

phoned

pho•net•ic

pho•net•i•cal•ly

pho•no•graph

pho•to

pho•to•copi•er

pho•to•ge•nic

pho•to•graph

pho•to•graphed

pho•tog•ra•pher

pho•to•graph•ic

pho•tos

phrase

phrased

phras•es

phys•i•cal

phys•i•cal•ly

phy•si•cian

phy•si•cians

phys•ics

phys•i•o•log•i•cal

phys•i•ol•o•gy

phy•sique

pi•a•nist

pi•ano

pick

picked

pick•le

pick•up

pic•nic

pic•ture

pic•tured

pie

piece

piec•es

pier

pig•ment

pile

piled

pil•fer

pill

pil•lar

pil•low

pi•lot

pin

pinch

pinched

pine

pink

pint

pi•o•neer

pipe

pit

pit•fall

piti•ful

pity

piv•ot•al

pla•cate

place

placed

place•ment

plac•id

pla•gia•rism

plague

plain

plain•ly

plain•tiff

plan

plane

plan•et

planned

plant

plant•ed	plu•ral	pomp•ous
plas•ma	plus	pond
plas•ter	pneu•mo•nia	pon•der
plas•tic	pock•et	pool
plate	po•di•um	poor
pla•teau	po•em	pop•u•lar
plat•form	po•et	pop•u•lar•i•ty
plat•i•num	po•et•ry	pop•u•late
plau•si•ble	point	pop•u•lat•ed
play	point•ed	pop•u•lates
played	poise	pop•u•la•tion
play•er	poi•son	porch
play•ful	poi•soned	port
plea	po•lice	por•ta•ble
plead	pol•i•cies	port•fo•lio
pleas•ant	pol•i•cy	por•tion
please	pol•i•cy•hold•er	por•tray
pleased	pol•ish	po•si•tion
pleas•es	po•lite	po•si•tioned
plea•sure	po•lite•ly	pos•i•tive
pledge	po•lit•i•cal	pos•sess
pledged	pol•i•ti•cian	pos•sessed
plen•ti•ful	pol•i•tics	pos•ses•sion
plen•ty	poll	pos•si•bil•i•ties
plight	pol•li•nate	pos•si•bil•i•ty
plot	pol•lute	pos•si•ble
plumb•er	pol•lu•tion	pos•si•bly

post	prag•mat•ic	pref•ace
post•age	praise	pre•fer
post•al	praised	pref•er•a•ble
post•ed	pray	pref•er•a•bly
post•grad•u•ate	preach	pref•er•ence
post•mark	preached	pref•er•enc•es
post•paid	pre•ar•range	pref•er•en•tial
post•pone	pre•cau•tion	pre•ferred
post•poned	pre•cede	preg•nan•cy
post•script	pre•ced•ed	preg•nant
pos•ture	pre•ce•dence	pre•judge
po•ta•to	prec•e•dent	prej•u•diced
po•ten•tial	pre•cious	pre•lim•i•nary
po•ten•tial•ly	pre•cise	pre•ma•ture
pot•pour•ri	pre•cise•ly	pre•med•i•tate
pound	pre•ci•sion	pre•mier
pour	pre•clude	prem•ise
poured	pre•co•cious	prem•is•es
pov•er•ty	pre•con•ceived	pre•mi•um
pow•der	pre•de•ter•mine	pre•oc•cu•pied
pow•er		pre•paid
pow•er•ful	pre•dic•a•ment	prep•a•ra•tion
pow•er•less	pre•dict	pre•pare
prac•ti•cal	pre•dict•able	pre•pared
prac•ti•cal•ly	pre•dic•tion	pre•pay
prac•tice	pre•dom•i•nant	pre•pay•ment
prac•ticed	pre•dom•i•nate	prep•o•si•tion

pre•req•ui•site

pre•scribe

pre•scrip•tion

pres•ence

pre•sent

pres•ent

pre•sen•ta•tion

pre•sen•ta•tions

pre•sent•ed

pres•ent•ly

pres•er•va•tion

pre•serve

pre•side

pres•i•den•cy

pres•i•dent

pres•i•den•tial

press

pressed

pres•sure

pres•sured

pres•tige

pres•ti•gious

pre•sume

pre•sumed

pre•sump•tion

pre•sump•tu•ous

pre•tend

pre•tense

pret•ty

pre•vent

pre•vent•ed

pre•ven•tion

pre•ven•tive

pre•view

pre•vi•ous

pre•vi•ous•ly

priced

price•less

pric•es

pride

priest

priest•hood

pri•mar•i•ly

pri•ma•ry

prim•i•tive

prince

prin•cess

prin•ci•pal

prin•ci•pal•ly

prin•ci•ple

prin•ci•ples

print

print•ed

print•er

print•out

pri•or

pri•or•i•ties

pri•or•i•ty

pris•on

pri•va•cy

pri•vate

pri•vate•ly

priv•i•lege

priv•i•leged

priv•i•leg•es

prob•a•ble

prob•a•bly

pro•bate

pro•ba•tion

probe

prob•lem

pro•ce•dur•al

pro•ce•dure

pro•ceed

pro•ceed•ed

pro•ceed•ings

pro•cess

pro•cessed

pro•cess•es

proc•la•ma•tion

pro•cras•ti•nate

pro•cure

pro•duce

pro•duced

pro•duc•er

pro•duc•es

prod•uct

pro•duc•tion

pro•duc•tiv•i•ty

prod•ucts

pro•fess

pro•fessed

pro•fes•sion

pro•fes•sion•al

pro•fes•sion•al•ly

pro•fes•sions

pro•fes•sor

pro•fi•cien•cy

pro•fi•cient

pro•file

prof•it

prof•it•able

prof•it•ed

pro•gram

pro•grammed

pro•gram•mer

prog•ress

pro•gress

pro•gressed

pro•hib•it

pro•hib•it•ed

proj•ect

pro•ject

pro•jec•tion

pro•long

pro•longed

prom•i•nence

prom•i•nent

prom•ise

prom•ised

prom•is•es

prom•is•so•ry

pro•mote

pro•mot•ed

pro•mo•tion

pro•mo•tion•al

prompt

prompt•ly

prompt•ness

pro•nate

prone

pro•noun

pro•nounce

pro•nounced

pro•nun•ci•a•tion

proof

proof•read

pro•pel

pro•pelled

prop•er

prop•er•ly

prop•er•ty

proph•e•cy

proph•et

pro•por•tion

pro•por•tion•al

pro•por•tion•ate

pro•pos•al

pro•pose

pro•posed

pro•pos•es

prop•o•si•tion

pro•pri•etor

pro•pri•etor•ship

prose

pros•e•cute

pros•e•cu•tion

pros•e•cu•tor

pros•pect

pros•per

pros•per•i•ty

pros•per•ous

pro•tect

pro•tect•ed

pro•tec•tion

pro•tein

pro•test

pro•test•ed

pro•tho•no•ta•ry

pro•to•col

pro•to•type

proud

proud•ly

prove

proved

prov•en

proves

pro•vide

pro•vid•ed

prov•ince

pro•vi•sion

pro•vi•sion•al

pro•vi•sions

pro•voke

prox•im•i•ty

proxy

pru•dent

pseud•onym

pso•ri•a•sis

psy•cho•log•i•cal

psy•chol•o•gy

psy•chot•ic

pub•lic

pub•li•ca•tion

pub•li•ca•tions

pub•lic•i•ty

pub•li•cize

pub•lic•ly

pub•lish

pub•lished

pub•lish•er

pub•lish•es

pull

pulled

pul•mo•nary

punc•tu•al

punc•tu•al•i•ty

punc•tu•ate

punc•tu•a•tion

pun•ish

pun•ished

pun•ish•ment

pu•ni•tive

pu•pil

pur•chase

pur•chased

pur•chas•es

pure

pure•ly

purge

pu•ri•fy

pu•ri•ty

pur•ple

pur•port

pur•pose

pur•pos•es

purse

pur•sue

pur•sues

pur•suit

push

push•es

put

puz•zle

pyr•a•mid

Q

qual•i•fi•ca•tion

qual•i•fi•ca•tions

qual•i•fied

qual•i•fies

qual•i•fy

qual•i•ties

qual•i•ty

quan•ti•ties

quan•ti•ty

quar•an•tine

quar•rel

quart

quar•ter

quar•ter•ly

quar•ters

quartz

queen

queer

quench

que•ries

que•ry

quest

ques•tion

ques•tion•able

ques•tioned

ques•tion•naire

ques•tion•naires

ques•tions

quick

quick•ly

quick•ness

qui•et

qui•et•ly

quit

quite

quiz

quo•rum

quo•ta

quo•ta•tion

quote

quot•ed

R

rab•bit

ra•bid

race

raced

ra•cial

ra•cial•ly

rac•ism

rac•ist

ra•dar

ra•di•al

ra•di•ant

ra•di•ate

ra•di•a•tion

rad•i•cal

rad•i•cal•ly

ra•dio

ra•dio•ac•tive

ra•di•us

raft

rage

raid

rail

rail•road

rail•way

rain

rain•coat

rain•fall

rain•storm

raise

raised

rai•sin

ral•ly

ram•i•fi•ca•tion

ran

ranch

ran•dom

range

rank

ran•som

rap•id

rap•id•ly

rap•port

rare

rare•ly

rar•i•ty

rate

rath•er

rat•i•fi•ca•tion

rat•i•fy

ra•tio

ra•tion

ra•tio•nal

ra•tio•nal•ize

ra•tio•nal•ly

rav•age

rav•en•ous

raw

ra•zor

reach

reached

reach•es

re•act

re•ac•tion

re•ac•ti•vate

read

read•er

read•er•ship

readi•ly

readi•ness

re•ad•just

re•ad•just•ment

re•ad•mit

ready

re•af•firm

re•al

re•al•ist

re•al•is•tic

re•al•i•ty

re•al•iza•tion

re•al•ize

re•al•ized

re•al•ly

realm

re•al•tor

re•al•ty

ream

reap

re•ap•pear

re•ap•pear•ance

rear

re•ar•range

rea•son

rea•son•able

rea•son•ably

rea•soned

re•as•sign

re•as•sur•ance

re•as•sured

re•bate

reb•el

re•bel

re•belled

re•bel•lion

re•bel•lious

re•bound

re•build

re•buke

re•but•tal

re•call

re•called

re•ca•pit•u•late

re•cede

re•ced•ed

re•ceipt

re•ceipts

re•ceiv•able

re•ceive

re•ceived

re•cent

re•cent•ly

re•cep•tion

re•cep•tive

re•cess

re•ces•sion

re•ces•sive

re•cip•i•ent

re•cip•ro•cal

re•cip•ro•cate

re•cip•ro•cat•ed

re•cit•al

rec•i•ta•tion

re•cite

re•cit•ed

reck•less

reck•on

re•claim

re•claimed

re•cline

re•clined

rec•og•ni•tion

rec•og•nize

rec•og•nized

rec•og•niz•es

rec•ol•lect

rec•om•mend

rec•om•men•da•tion

rec•om•men•da•tions

rec•om•mend•ed

rec•on•cile

rec•on•cil•i•a•tion

re•con•nais•sance

re•con•sid•er

re•con•sid•ered

re•con•struct

re•cord

rec•ord

re•cord•ed

re•cord•er

re•cord•ings

re•coup

re•course

re•cov•er

re•cov•ery

rec•re•ation

re•crim•i•na•tion

re•cruit

re•cruit•ed

re•cruit•ment

rect•an•gle

rect•an•gu•lar

rec•ti•fy

re•cu•per•ate

re•cur

re•curred

re•cur•rence

re•cy•cle

red

re•deemed

re•demp•tion

re•di•rect

re•dis•cov•er

re•duce

re•duced

re•duc•es

re•duc•tion

re•dun•dant

red•wood	re•fus•al	reg•u•late
re•elect	re•fuse	reg•u•lat•ed
re•en•act	re•fused	reg•u•lates
re•en•try	re•fus•es	reg•u•la•tion
re•fer	re•fute	reg•u•la•tions
ref•er•ence	re•fut•ed	re•ha•bil•i•tate
ref•er•enc•es	re•gain	re•ha•bil•i•ta•tion
re•ferred	re•gained	re•hash
re•fill	re•gard	re•hears•al
re•fi•nance	re•gard•ed	re•hearse
re•fine	re•gard•less	re•hearsed
re•fined	re•gen•er•ate	reign
re•flect	reg•i•ment	re•im•burse
re•flect•ed	re•gion	rein
re•flec•tion	re•gion•al	rein•deer
re•flex	re•gion•al•ly	re•in•force
re•form	reg•is•ter	re•in•forced
re•formed	reg•is•tered	re•in•sert
re•frain	reg•is•tra•tion	re•in•state
re•frained	re•gret	re•in•stat•ed
re•fresh	re•gret•ful	re•in•vest
re•freshed	re•gret•ful•ly	re•is•sue
re•fresh•ment	re•gret•ta•ble	re•it•er•ate
re•frig•er•ate	re•gret•ted	re•ject
ref•uge		re•ject•ed
re•fund	reg•u•lar	re•jec•tion
re•fund•ed	reg•u•lar•ly	re•joice

re•joiced

re•join

re•ju•ve•nate

re•ju•ve•na•tion

re•kin•dle

re•lapse

re•late

re•lat•ed

re•la•tion

re•la•tions

re•la•tion•ship

re•la•tion•ships

rel•a•tive

rel•a•tive•ly

rel•a•tives

re•lax

re•lax•ation

re•laxed

re•lax•es

re•lay

re•layed

re•lease

re•leased

re•leas•es

re•lent

rel•e•vance

rel•e•vant

re•li•able

re•li•ance

re•lief

re•lieve

re•li•gion

re•li•gious

re•lin•quish

re•lin•quished

re•live

re•lo•cate

re•lo•ca•ted

re•lo•ca•tion

re•luc•tance

re•luc•tant

re•luc•tant•ly

re•ly

re•main

re•main•der

re•mained

re•make

re•mark

re•mark•able

re•marks

re•mar•ry

re•me•di•al

rem•e•dy

re•mem•ber

re•mem•bered

re•mem•brance

re•mind

re•mind•ed

re•mind•er

rem•i•nis•cence

rem•i•nis•cent

re•mit

re•mit•tance

re•mit•tanc•es

re•mod•el

re•mod•eled

re•mote

re•mov•able

re•mov•al

re•move

re•moved

re•mu•ner•ate

re•mu•ner•a•tion

re•nais•sance

ren•der

ren•dered

ren•dez•vous

re•ne•go•ti•ate

re•new

re•new•al

re•newed

re•nounce

re•nounced

ren••o•vate

ren••o•vat•ed

ren••o•va•tion

rent

rent•al

rent•ed

re••or•der

re••or•ga•ni•za•tion

re••or•ga•nize

re•pair

re•paired

re•pay

re•pay•ment

re•peat

re•peat•ed

re•peat•ed•ly

re•pel

re•pel•lent

re•pent

rep•er•toire

rep•e•ti•tion

rep•e•ti•tious

re•pet•i•tive

re•place

re•placed

re•place•ment

re•plen•ish

rep•li•ca

re•plied

re•ply

re•port

re•port•ed

re•port•er

re•ports

re•pos•sess

rep•re•sent

rep•re•sen•ta•tion

rep•re•sen•ta•tive

rep•re•sen•ta•tives

rep•re•sent•ed

rep•re•sents

re•prieve

rep•ri•mand

re•print

re•pro•duce

re•pro•duc•tion

re•pub•lic

re•pulse

re•pul•sive

rep•u•ta•ble

rep•u•ta•tion

re•quest

re•quest•ed

re•quests

re•quire

re•quired

re•quire•ment

re•quire•ments

re•quires

req•ui•si•tion

re•sale

re•scind

re•scind•ed

res•cue

re•search

re•search•er

re•sem•blance

re•sem•ble

re•sent

re•sent•ed

re•sent•ful

re•sent•ment

res•er•va•tion

res•er•va•tions

re•serve

re•served

re•serves

re•set

re•side

re•sid•ed

res•i•dence

res•i•dent

res•i•den•tial

re•sid•u•al

res•i•due

re•sign

res•ig•na•tion

re•signed

re•sil•ient

re•sist

re•sis•tance

re•sis•tant

re•sist•ed

res•o•lu•tion

re•solve

re•sort

re•sort•ed

re•source

re•source•ful

re•sourc•es

re•spect

re•spect•able

re•spect•ed

re•spect•ful

re•spec•tive

re•spec•tive•ly

re•spi•ra•to•ry

re•spond

re•spond•ed

re•spon•dent

re•sponse

re•spons•es

re•spon•si•bil•i•ties

re•spon•si•bil•i•ty

re•spon•si•ble

rest

re•state

re•state•ment

res•tau•rant

rest•ed

rest•ful

rest•less

rest•less•ness

re•store

re•stored

re•strain

re•strict

re•stric•tion

re•stric•tive

re•stric•tions

re•sult

re•sul•ted

re•sults

ré•sumé

re•su•me

re•sumed

re•tail

re•tailed

re•tail•er

re•tain

re•tained

re•take

re•tal•i•ate

re•tal•i•at•ed

re•tal•i•a•tion

re•tard

re•tard•ed

re•ten•tion

re•think

ret•i•na

re•tire

re•tired

re•tire•ment

re•tort

re•tract

re•tract•ed

re•trac•tion

re•treat

re•treat•ed

re•trench

re•triev•al

re•trieve

ret•ro•ac•tive

ret•ro•spect

re•turn

re•turned

re•union

re•unite

re•use

re•veal

re•vealed

rev•eil•le

rev•e•la•tion

re•venge

rev•e•nue

re•vere

rev•er•end

re•ver•sal

re•verse

re•versed

re•vers•ible

re•vert

re•view

re•viewed

re•vise

re•vised

re•vi•sion

re•viv•al

re•vo•ca•tion

re•voke

re•voked

re•volt

rev•o•lu•tion

rev•o•lu•tion•ary

rev•o•lu•tion•ize

re•volve

re•ward

re•ward•ed

re•wards

re•write

re•writ•ten

rhet•o•ric

rhyme

rhymed

rhythm

rib•bon

rice

rich•est

rich•ly

ride

ridge

rid•i•cule

ri•dic•u•lous

right

righ•teous

right•ful

rig•id

ri•gid•i•ty

rig•or

rig•or•ous

ring

rinse

ri•ot

ri•ots

ripe

rip•en

rise

ris•en

ris•es

risk

risked

rite

rites

rit•u•al

ri•val

ri•val•ry

riv•er

road

road•way

roam

roar

roast

rob

robbed

rob•bery

robe

ro•bot

ro•bust

rock

rock•et

rode

role

roles

roll

ro•mance

ro•man•tic

ro•man•ti•cize

roof

room

room•mate

root

rope

rose

ros•es

ro•tate

ro•tat•ed

ro•ta•tion

rote

rough

round

route

rou•tine

roy•al

roy•al•ties

roy•al•ty

rub•ber

rude

rude•ly

rude•ness

ru•di•men•ta•ry

ru•in

ru•ined

rule

ruled

rul•er

rules

rul•ings

ru•mor

ru•mored

run

rung

run•way

rup•ture

rup•tured

ru•ral

rush

rushed

rush•es

Rus•sian

ruth•less

s

sab•bat•i•cal

sab•o•tage

sa•cred

sac•ri•fice

sad

sad•ly

sad•ness

safe

safe•guard

safe•keep•ing

safe•ly

saf•est

safe•ty

said

sail

saint

sal•a•ried

sal•a•ries

sal•a•ry

sale

sales

sales•clerk

sales•man

sales•men

sales•peo•ple

sales•per•son

sales•wom•an

sa•lient

salt

sa•lute

sal•va•tion

same

sam•ple

sam•ples

sanc•tion

sanc•tioned

sand

sand•wich

sane

sang

san•i•tary

san•i•ty

sank

sar•casm

sar•cas•tic

sat

sat•ire

sat•is•fac•tion

sat•is•fac•to•ri•ly

sat•is•fac•to•ry

sat•is•fied

sat•is•fies

sat•is•fy

sat•is•fy•ing•ly

sat•u•rate

sat•u•rat•ed

sat•u•ra•tion

Sat•ur•day

sauce

save

saved

saves

sav•ings

sa•vory

saw

say

say•ings

says

scald

scale

scan

scan•dal

scarce

scar•ci•ty

scare

scared

sce•nar•io

scene

scen•ery

sce•nic

scent

scent•ed

sched•ule

sched•uled

sche•mat•ic

scheme

schizo•phre•nia

schizo•phren•ic

schol•ar

schol•ar•ship

scho•las•tic

school

schools

sci•ence

sci•en•tif•ic

sci•en•tist

scis•sors

scold

sco•li•o•sis

scope

score

scored

scorn

scout

scrape

scratch

scratched

scream

screamed

screen

script

scrub

scru•pu•lous

scru•ti•nize

sculp•tor

sculp•ture

seal

sealed

seam

sea•port

search

searched

search•es

sea•son

sea•son•able

sea•son•al

sea•son•al•ly

sea•soned

sea•son•ings

seat

seat•ed

se•ba•ceous

se•clude

se•clud•ed

sec•ond

sec•ond•ary

se•cre•cy

se•cret

sec•re•tari•al

sec•re•tar•ies

sec•re•tary

se•crete

se•cre•tion

sect

sec•tion

sec•tion•al

sec•tor

se•cure

se•cured

se•cure•ly

se•cu•ri•ties

se•cu•ri•ty

se•date

se•date•ly

se•da•tion

sed•a•tive

sed•i•ment

se•duce

se•duced

se•duc•tive

see	self-de•fense	send•er
seek	self-de•struct	sends
seem	self-de•ter•mi•na•tion	se•nile
seemed	self-gov•erned	se•nil•i•ty
seem•ing•ly	self-help	se•nior
seen	self-in•ter•est	se•nior•i•ty
seg•ment	self•ish	sen•sa•tion
seg•re•gate	self•ish•ly	sense
seg•re•gat•ed	self•ish•ness	sense•less
seg•re•ga•tion	self-made	sens•es
seize	self-re•li•ance	sen•si•bil•i•ty
seized	self-sat•is•fied	sen•si•ble
sei•zure	self-suf•fi•cient	sen•si•tive
sel•dom	self-sup•port	sen•si•tiv•i•ty
se•lect	sell	sen•so•ry
se•lect•ed	sem•blance	sen•su•al
se•lec•tion	se•mes•ter	sent
se•lec•tive	semi•an•nu•al	sen•tence
self	semi•co•lon	sen•ti•ment
self-ad•dress	semi•con•scious	sep•a•rate
self-ad•dressed	semi•fin•al•ist	sep•a•rat•ed
self-as•sur•ance	semi•month•ly	sep•a•rate•ly
self-as•sured	sem•i•nar	sep•a•rates
self-cen•tered	semi•week•ly	sep•a•ra•tion
self-con•fi•dence	sen•ate	Sep•tem•ber
self-con•fi•dent	sen•a•tor	se•quel
self-con•trol	send	se•quence

se•quen•tial	sew	shocked
se•quen•tial•ly	shade	shoe
se•ques•ter	shake	shoes
ser•e•nade	shall	shoot
se•rene	shape	shop
se•ren•i•ty	shapes	shop•lift•er
ser•geant	share	shopped
se•ri•al	share•hold•er	short•age
se•ries	sharp	short•change
se•ri•ous	sharp•ly	short•com•ings
se•ri•ous•ly	she	short•en
ser•vant	sheep	short•er
serve	sheep•ish	short•est
served	sheep•ish•ly	short•hand
ser•vice	sheet	short•ly
ser•viced	shelf	shot
ser•vic•es	shel•ter	should
serv•ings	shift	shout
ses•sion	shift•ed	shout•ed
ses•sions	shine	show
set	ship	show•case
sets	ship•ment	showed
set•tle	shipped	show•er
set•tled	ships	show•ered
set•tle•ment	shirt	show•ings
set•tle•ments	shirts	shown
sev•er•al	shock	show•room

shrewd

shrimp

shrine

shrink•age

shrub

shrub•bery

shut

shy

shy•ly

shy•ness

sick

side

sid•ed

siege

sieve

sift

sigh

sighed

sight

sig•nal

sig•na•ture

signed

sig•nif•i•cance

sig•nif•i•cant

sig•nif•i•cant•ly

sig•ni•fy

si•lence

si•lent

sil•ver

sim•i•lar

sim•i•lar•i•ty

sim•i•lar•ly

sim•ple

sim•pler

sim•plest

sim•plic•i•ty

sim•pli•fied

sim•pli•fy

sim•ply

sim•u•late

sin•cere

sin•cere•ly

sin•cer•est

sin•cer•i•ty

sing

sin•gle

sin•gu•lar

sink

sir

sis•ter

sis•ter-in-law

sit

site

sit•u•ate

sit•u•at•ed

sit•u•a•tion

siz•able

size

siz•es

skel•e•ton

skep•ti•cal

sketch

ski

skin

skip

skirt

skull

sky

slain

slan•der

slang

slant

sleep

slept

slight

slight•est

slight•ly

slip•page

slipped

slo•gan

slow

slow•er

slow•est

slow•ly

slump

small

smart

smash

smear

smell

smile

smoke

smooth

smooth•er

smooth•est

smooth•ly

smooth•ness

snow

snowed

snowy

so

soap

so•cia•ble

so•cial

so•cial•ly

so•ci•ety

so•ci•ol•o•gy

so•da

so•di•um

soft

soft•en

soft•ware

soil

so•lar

sold

sole

sole•ly

sol•emn

so•lic•it

so•lic•i•ta•tion

so•lic•it•ed

so•lic•i•tor

sol•id

so•lil•o•quy

sol•i•tary

so•lu•tion

solve

solved

sol•ven•cy

sol•vent

some

some•body

some•how

some•one

some•thing

some•time

some•times

some•what

some•where

son

song

son-in-law

soon

soon•er

soothe

so•phis•ti•cat•ed

soph•o•more

sor•row

sor•ry

sort

sort•ed

sought

sound

sound•ed

sound•ly

source

sourc•es

south

south•east

south•east•ern

south•er•ly

south•ern

south•west	spec•tac•u•lar	spon•ta•ne•ous•ly
sou•ve•nir	spec•ta•tor	sport
space	spec•u•late	sports•wear
spac•es	spec•u•lat•ed	spot
spa•cious	spec•u•la•tion	spouse
span	spec•u•la•tive	spread
spar•ing•ly	spec•u•la•tor	spring
sparse	speech	square
speak	speech•less	square•ly
speak•er	speed	squeeze
speak•ers	speed•i•ly	sta•bil•i•ty
speaks	spend	sta•bi•lize
spe•cial	spent	sta•bi•lized
spe•cial•ist	spice	sta•ble
spe•cial•ists	spin-off	stack
spe•cial•iza•tion	spir•it	staff
spe•cial•ize	spite	stage
spe•cial•ized	splen•did	stag•ger
spe•cial•iz•es	splurge	stag•gered
spe•cials	spoil	stag•nant
spe•cial•ty	spoiled	stain
spe•cif•ic	spoke	stained
spe•cif•i•cal•ly	spo•ken	stair
spec•i•fi•ca•tion	spon•sor	stake
spec•i•fi•ca•tions	spon•sored	stale
spec•i•fied	spon•sor•ship	stam•i•na
spec•i•fy	spon•ta•ne•ous	stamp

stand

stan•dard

stan•dard•ize

stan•dards

stand•ings

stand•point

star

start

start•ed

state

stat•ed

state•ly

state•ment

state•ments

states

sta•tion

sta•tion•ary

sta•tioned

sta•tio•nery

sta•tions

sta•tis•tic

sta•tis•ti•cal

sta•tis•tics

stat•ue

sta•tus

stat•ute

stat•u•to•ry

stay

stayed

stays

steadi•ly

steady

steam

steam•ship

steel

sten•cil

ste•nog•ra•pher

steno•graph•ic

step

ste•reo

ster•ile

ste•ril•ize

stiff

still

stim•u•late

stim•u•lat•ed

stim•u•la•tion

stip•u•late

stip•u•lat•ed

stip•u•lates

stip•u•la•tion

stock

stock•bro•ker

stocked

stock•hold•er

stocks

stole

stol•en

stom•ach

stood

stop

stop•page

stopped

stor•age

store

stored

store•room

stores

sto•ries

storm

sto•ry

straight

straight•en

straight•ened

straight•for•ward

strain

strange

strang•er

stra•te•gic

strat•e•gy

stray

street	sub•di•vide	sub•stan•dard
streets	sub•di•vi•sion	sub•stan•tial
strength	sub•due	sub•stan•tial•ly
strength•en	sub•ject	sub•stan•ti•ate
strength•ened	sub•ject•ed	sub•stan•ti•at•ed
stress	sub•jec•tive	sub•sti•tute
stretch	sub•jec•tive•ly	sub•sti•tut•ed
strict	sub•jects	sub•sti•tutes
stride	sub•lease	sub•sti•tu•tion
strike	sub•leased	sub•tle
strikes	sub•leas•es	sub•tract
string	sub•let	sub•urb
strong	sub•merge	sub•ur•ban
strong•ly	sub•mit	sub•urbs
struc•ture	sub•mit•ted	sub•way
struc•tured	sub•or•di•nate	suc•ceed
stub•born	sub•poe•na	suc•cess
stu•dent	sub•poe•naed	suc•cess•ful
stud•ied	sub•scribe	suc•ces•sive
stud•ies	sub•scribed	suc•ces•sor
stu•dio	sub•scrib•er	suc•cinct
study	sub•scribes	such
stur•dy	sub•scrip•tion	sud•den
style	sub•se•quent	sud•den•ly
styl•ish	sub•se•quent•ly	sue
styl•ist	sub•si•dy	suf•fer
sub•con•tract	sub•stance	suf•fered

suf•fice

suf•fi•cient

sug•gest

sug•gest•ed

sug•ges•tion

sug•ges•tions

sug•gests

suit

suit•able

suite

sum

sum•ma•rize

sum•ma•rized

sum•ma•ry

sum•mon

sum•moned

sum•mons

sun

Sun•day

su•perb

su•per•fi•cial

su•per•in•ten•dent

su•pe•ri•or

su•pe•ri•ors

su•per•sede

su•per•sed•ed

su•per•vise

su•per•vised

su•per•vis•es

su•per•vi•sion

su•per•vi•sor

sup•per

sup•ple•ment

sup•ple•men•tal

sup•ple•men•ta•ry

sup•ple•ments

sup•plied

sup•pli•er

sup•plies

sup•ply

sup•port

sup•port•ed

sup•pose

sup•posed

su•preme

sure

sure•ly

sur•face

sur•geon

sur•gery

sur•gi•cal

sur•mise

sur•name

sur•pass

sur•plus

sur•prise

sur•prised

sur•pris•es

sur•pris•ing•ly

sur•ren•der

sur•ren•dered

sur•ro•gate

sur•round

sur•round•ings

sur•vey

sur•veyed

sur•veys

sur•viv•al

sur•vive

sus•cep•ti•ble

sus•pect

sus•pect•ed

sus•pend

sus•pend•ed

sus•pense

sus•pi•cion

sus•pi•cious

sus•tain

sus•tained

sweat•er

sweet

swell

swept

swift

swift•ly

swim

switch

syl•la•ble

sym•bol

sym•bol•ic

sym•bol•ize

sym•pa•thet•ic

sym•pa•thize

sym•pa•thy

symp•tom

syn•on•y•mous

syn•the•sis

syn•the•size

sys•tem

sys•tem•at•ic

sys•tems

T

tab

ta•ble

ta•bled

tab•u•late

tab•u•lat•ed

tab•u•lates

tab•u•la•tion

tact

tact•ful

tact•ful•ly

tac•tics

tai•lor

tai•lored

take

tak•en

takes

tal•ent

tal•ent•ed

tal•ents

talk

talked

tall

tall•est

tal•ly

tam•per

tan•gi•ble

tan•ta•mount

tape

tar•get

tar•iff

task

taste

taught

tax

tax•able

tax•a•tion

taxed

tax•es

taxi

tea

teach

teach•er

team

team•work

tech•ni•cal

tech•ni•cian

tech•nique

tech•niques

tech•no•log•i•cal

tech•nol•o•gy

te•dious

teeth	ten·ta·tive	thanked
tele·cast	term	thank·ful
tele·gram	termed	thank·ing
tele·graph	ter·mi·nal	thanks·giv·ing
tele·phone	ter·mi·nate	that
tele·phoned	ter·mi·nat·ed	the
tele·vise	ter·mi·na·tion	the·ater
tele·vi·sion	ter·mi·nol·o·gy	theft
tell	terms	their
tell·er	ter·ri·ble	theirs
tem·per	ter·ri·bly	them
tem·per·a·ment	ter·rif·ic	theme
tem·per·a·men·tal	ter·ri·fy	them·selves
	ter·ri·to·ries	then
tem·per·a·ture	ter·ri·to·ry	the·o·ries
tem·po·rari·ly	test	the·o·ry
tem·po·rary	test·ed	there
tempt	tes·ti·fied	there·af·ter
temp·ta·tion	tes·ti·fy	there·by
tempt·ed	tes·ti·mo·ni·al	there·fore
ten·ant	tes·ti·mo·ny	there·in
tend	tests	there·up·on
tend·ed	text	these
ten·den·cy	text·book	they
ten·der	tex·ture	thick
ten·der·ly	than	thief
tense	thank	thin

thing

things

think

think•ing

thinks

this

thor•ough

thor•ough•ly

thor•ough•ness

those

though

thought

thought•ful

thought•ful•ly

thought•less

thoughts

threat•en

threw

thrill

thrilled

thrive

through

through•out

throw

thrown

throws

Thurs•day

thus

tick•et

tick•ets

tie

tied

time

timed

time•ly

time•piece

times

tim•id

tim•ings

tire

tired

tires

ti•tle

ti•tled

ti•tles

to

to•day

toe

to•geth•er

to•ken

told

tol•er•a•ble

tol•er•ant

tol•er•ate

tol•er•at•ed

toll

to•mor•row

ton

tone

to•night

too

took

tool

top

top•ic

tor•ment

tort

toss

to•tal

to•taled

to•tal•ly

touch

touched

touch•es

tough

tough•er

tough•est

tour

toured

tour•ist

to•ward

to•wards	trans•act•ed	trans•pose
town	trans•ac•tion	trap
towns	tran•scend	trav•el
town•ship	tran•scribe	trav•eled
tox•ic	tran•script	trav•el•er
toy	tran•scrip•tion	tread
toys	trans•fer	trea•sure
trace	trans•fer•al	trea•sur•er
traced	trans•ferred	trea•sury
trac•es	trans•fers	treat
track	trans•form	treat•ment
trade	trans•for•ma•tion	tree
trad•ed	trans•formed	trees
trade•mark	trans•fuse	tre•men•dous
tra•di•tion	trans•fu•sion	tre•men•dous•ly
tra•di•tion•al	tran•sis•tor	trend
tra•di•tion•al•ly	tran•sit	tres•pass
traf•fic	trans•late	tri•al
trag•e•dy	trans•lat•ed	tri•bune
trag•ic	trans•la•tion	trib•ute
trail	trans•mis•sion	trick
train	trans•mit	tried
trained	trans•mit•ted	tries
train•ees	trans•par•ent	tri•ple
trait	trans•plant	tri•umph
tran•quil	trans•port	tri•um•phant
trans•act	trans•por•ta•tion	triv•i•al

trop•i•cal

trou•ble

trou•bled

trou•bles

trou•ble•some

truck

true

tru•ly

trust

trust•ed

trust•ee

trust•wor•thy

truth

truth•ful

truth•ful•ly

truth•ful•ness

tube

tu•ber•cu•lo•sis

Tues•day

tu•ition

tu•mor

tuna

tune

tun•nel

turn

turned

turn•out

turn•over

twice

two

type

typed

type•writ•ers

type•writ•ten

typ•i•cal

typ•i•cal•ly

typ•i•fy

typ•ist

ty•po•graph•i•cal

U

ug•ly

ul•ti•mate

ul•ti•mate•ly

ul•ti•ma•tum

un•able

un•ac•cept•able

un•af•fect•ed

unan•i•mous

un•an•swered

un•au•tho•rized

un•avail•able

un•avoid•able

un•be•liev•able

un•bi•ased

un•cer•tain

un•claimed

un•com•mon

un•con•di•tion•al

un•con•firmed

un•con•ven•tion•al

un•de•cid•ed

un•der

un•der•es•ti•mate

un•der•es•ti•mat•ed

un•der•go

un•der•line

un•der•neath

un•der•rate

un•der•stand

un•der•stand•able

un•der•stand•ings

un•der•state

un•der•stat•ed

un•der•state•ment

un•der•stood

un•der•take

un•der•tak•ing

un•de•sir•able

un•de•vel•oped

un•dis•put•ed

un•doubt•ed•ly

un•easy

un•em•ployed

un•em•ploy•ment

un•even

un•ex•pect•ed

un•fair

un•fore•seen

un•for•tu•nate

un•for•tu•nate•ly

un•grate•ful

un•hap•py

uni•fied

uni•form

uni•fy

un•im•por•tant

union

unions

unique

unit

unite

unit•ed

units

uni•ver•sal

uni•ver•si•ty

un•just

un•just•ly

un•kind

un•know•ing•ly

un•known

un•law•ful

un•less

un•like

un•like•li•hood

un•lucky

un•no•ticed

un•paid

un•planned

un•pleas•ant

un•ques•tion•able

un•rea•son•able

un•re•lat•ed

un•re•li•able

un•safe

un•sat•is•fac•to•ry

un•seen

un•self•ish

un•suc•cess•ful

un•sure

un•til

un•to

un•used

un•usu•al

un•usu•al•ly

un•will•ing

un•will•ing•ly

un•wise

up

up•date

up•dat•ed

up•grade

up•grad•ed

up•keep

up•on

up•per	**v**	ver•i•fi•ca•tion
up•set		ver•i•fy
up•state	va•can•cy	ver•sa•tile
up•ward	va•cant	ver•sion
ur•ban	va•cat•ed	ver•sus
urge	va•ca•tion	very
urged	vac•ci•nate	vest
ur•gen•cy	vague	vet•er•an
ur•gent	vain	ve•to
us	val•id	via
us•able	val•i•date	vi•a•ble
us•age	valu•able	vi•brant
use	val•ue	vice
used	val•ued	vice pres•i•dent
use•ful	vari•able	vi•cin•i•ty
use•less	var•ied	vic•tim
uses	va•ri•ety	vic•to•ry
usu•al	var•i•ous	vid•eo•tape
usu•al•ly	vary	view
usu•ry	vast	viewed
util•i•ties	vault	vil•lage
util•i•ty	ve•hi•cle	vine
uti•li•za•tion	ven•dor	vi•o•late
uti•lize	ven•ture	vi•o•la•tion
ut•most	ver•bal	vi•o•lent
	ver•dict	vir•tu•al•ly
	verge	vi•rus

W

vis•i•bil•i•ty	
vis•i•ble	
vi•sion	
vis•it	
vis•it•ed	
vis•i•tor	
vi•su•al	
vi•su•al•ize	
vi•tal	
viv•id	
vo•cal	
vo•ca•tion	
vo•ca•tion•al	
voice	
voiced	
void	
void•ed	
volt•age	
vol•ume	
vol•un•tari•ly	
vol•un•tary	
vol•un•teer	
vote	
vot•ed	
vow	
vowed	
vul•ner•a•ble	

wage	
wag•es	
wait	
wait•ed	
waive	
waived	
waiv•er	
wake	
walk	
walked	
want	
want•ed	
wants	
ward	
ware•house	
warm	
warn•ings	
war•rant	
war•rant•ed	
war•ran•ty	
was	
wash	
washed	
wasn't	
waste	

watch	
watched	
wa•ter	
wax	
way	
we	
weak	
weak•en	
weak•ened	
weak•er	
weak•est	
weak•ness	
wealth	
wealthy	
wear	
weath•er	
Wednes•day	
week	
week•day	
week•end	
week•ly	
weeks	
weigh	
weight	
wel•come	
wel•comed	
wel•fare	

well	whose	with•draw•al
well-known	why	with•drawn
went	wide	with•drew
were	wide•ly	with•held
west	wide•spread	with•hold
west•ern	wid•ow	with•hold•ings
what	width	with•in
what•ev•er	wife	with•out
what•so•ev•er	wild	with•stand
when	will	with•stood
when•ev•er	will•ing•ly	wit•ness
where	will•ing•ness	wit•nessed
where•as	win•dow	wom•an
where•by	windy	wom•en
where•in	win•ner	won
where•up•on	wins	won•der
wher•ev•er	win•ter	won•dered
wheth•er	wipe	won•der•ful
which	wire	won't
which•ev•er	wis•dom	wood
while	wise•ly	wood•en
who	wish	wool
who•ev•er	wished	word
whole	wish•es	work
whole•sale	wish•ful	work•able
whom	with	work•book
whom•ev•er	with•draw	worked

work•er ⌣

work•ers ⌣

works ⌣

world ⌢

world•ly ⌢

world•wide ⌢

worn ⌢

wor•ried 2⌢

wor•ry 2⌢

worse 2⌢

worst 2⌢

worth ⌢

worth•less ⌢

worth•while ⌢

wor•thy ⌢

would /

wouldn't /

wrap ⌣

wreck ⌣

write ⌢

writ•er ⌢

writes ⌢

writ•ings ⌢

writ•ten ⌢

wrong ⌣

wrong•ful ⌣

wrote ⌣

X

Xe•rox ⌢

X ray 2⌢

Y

yard ⌢

yawn ⌢

year ⌢

year•book ⌢

year•ly ⌢

years ⌢

yeast ⌢

yell ⌢

yel•low ⌢

yes 9

yes•ter•day ⌢

yet 6

yield ⌢

yield•ed ⌢

you ⌢

young ⌢

your ⌢

yours ⌢

your•self ⌢

your•selves ⌢

youth ⌢

youth•ful ⌢

Z

zeal•ous

ze•ro

zone

zoned

zoo

zo••ol••o•gy

PART 2

BRIEF FORMS

a	anywhere	circumstances
about	appropriate	communicate
accompany	appropriately	communicated
acknowledge	appropriation	communication
acknowledged	are	communications
acknowledges	at	companies
acknowledgment	be	company
advantage	became	convenience
advantages	because	convenient
advertise	before	conveniently
advertised	began	correspond
advertises	being	corresponded
advertising	believe	correspondence
afford	beside	correspondent
afforded	between	corresponds
after	business	could
afternoon	businesses	depart
am	businesslike	departed
an	but	department
and	by	difficult
anniversary	can	difficulties
any	cannot	difficulty
anybody	character	direct
anyone	characters	directed
anything	circular	direction
anytime	circulars	directly
anyway	circumstance	director

disadvantage	experiences	ideas
doctor	extraordinary	immediate
doctors	for	immediately
Dr.	force	importance
during	forced	important
electric	forget	in
electrical	forgive	include
electricity	form	included
electronic	forms	includes
electronically	from	including
enclose	general	inclusion
enclosed	generally	inconvenience
encloses	gentleman	inconvenient
enclosure	gentlemen	inconveniently
envelope	glad	incorporate
envelopes	gladly	incorporated
equip	good	inform
equipment	goods	informed
equipped	govern	insurance
equivalent	governed	insure
ever	government	insured
every	have	insuring
everywhere	his	is
executive	hour	it
executives	however	manufacture
experience	I	manufactured
experienced	idea	manufacturer

manufactures	opportunity	party
memorandum	order	present
morning	ordered	presentation
mornings	ordering	presentations
Mr.	orders	presented
Mrs.	ordinarily	presently
Ms.	ordinary	privilege
never	organization	privileges
nevertheless	organize	probable
newspaper	organized	probably
newspapers	organizes	product
next	our	production
not	out	productivity
nothing	outcome	products
object	outside	program
objected	outstanding	programmed
objection	over	programmer
objective	overhead	programming
objects	overlook	programs
of	overnight	progress
office	part	progressed
offices	parted	progressive
once	particular	property
one	particularly	public
opinion	partly	publication
opinions	partner	publications
opportunities	parts	publicly

publish	reluctantly	soon
published	representative	sooner
publishes	represented	speak
quantities	request	speakers
quantity	requested	speaks
question	requesting	state
questionable	requests	stated
questioned	responsibility	states
questionnaire	responsible	statistical
questions	satisfactory	statistics
recognition	satisfied	street
recognize	satisfies	streets
recognized	satisfy	subject
recognizes	satisfying	subjected
recommend	send	subjects
recommendation	sending	success
recommendations	sends	successes
recommended	several	suggest
recommends	short	suggested
regard	shortage	suggestion
regarded	shorthand	suggests
regarding	shortly	than
regardless	should	thank
regular	significance	thanking
regularly	significant	thanks
reluctance	significantly	that
reluctant	sometime	the

their

them

there

they

thing

things

think

thinking

thinks

this

throughout

time

timed

timely

under

underneath

understand

understood

unusual

usual

usually

valuable

value

valued

values

very

was

well

were

what

whatever

when

whenever

where

which

will

willing

wish

wished

wishes

wishful

with

within

without

won

work

worked

worker

world

worldly

worldwide

worth

worthless

worthwhile

would

yesterday

you

your

PART

3

PHRASES

about the	by this time	do so
about them	by which	do you
about this	by you	do you know
about you	by your	do you think
about your	can be	does not
after that	can have	every month
after the	can you	for me
are in	cannot be	for my
are not	cannot have	for our
as soon as	check up	for that
as soon as possible	Cordially yours	for the
as the	could be	for this
as you	could be able	for us
as you are	could have	for you
as you know	could have been	for your
as you will	could not	from our
as your	could not be	from the
at this	Dear Madam	from you
at this time	Dear Miss	from your
be able	Dear Mr.	had been
be glad	Dear Mrs.	had been able
been able	Dear Ms.	had not
being able	Dear Sir	had not been
by that time	did not	has been
by the	did not have	has been able
by the time	do not	has not been
by this	do not have	has not been able

have been

have been able

have had

have not

have not been

have not been able

he will

he will be

he will have

he will not

here are

here is

I am

I am glad

I am sure

I can

I can be

I can have

I cannot

I cannot be

I cannot have

I could

I could be

I could have

I could not

I did

I did not

I do

I do not

I do not think

I have

I have been

I have been able

I have had

I have not

I have not been

I have not been able

I hope

I hope that

I hope that the

I hope the

I hope you are

I hope you will

I know

I may

I may be

I may have

I might

I might be

I might have

I need

I should

I should be

I should have

I think

I was

I will

I will be

I will be able

I will be glad

I will have

I will not

I will not be

I will not be able

I would

I would be

I would have

I would not

I would not be

if the

if you

if you are

if you can

if you can be

if you cannot

if you have

if you will

if you would

if your

in it

in order

in our	might have	one of these
in that	might have been	send the
in the	might not	send us
in this	might not be	send you
in which	might not be able	send your
is in	must be	sending us
is not	must be able	sending you
is the	next month	several months
is there	next time	should be
is this	next year	should be able
it has been	of course	should have
it is	of his	should have been
it was	of our	should not be
it will	of the	Sincerely yours
it will be	of them	some of our
it will have	of these	some of the
it will not	of this	some of them
it will not be	of you	thank you
let me	of your	thank you for
let us	on it	thank you for the
let us have	on our	thank you for your
let us know	on the	thank you for your letter
may be	on this	
may be able	on which	thank you for your order
may have	one of our	that are
might be	one of the	that the
might be able	one of them	that will

that will be

there are

there is

there was

there will

there will be

they are

they are not

they will

they will be

they will be able

they will have

they will not

this is

this is the

this may

this will

this will be

to be

to be able

to do

to do so

to do the

to have

to know

to make

to me

to take

to the

to us

to you

to your

up to date

Very cordially yours

very much

Very sincerely yours

Very truly yours

we are

we are not

we can

we can be

we can have

we cannot

we cannot be

we could

we could be

we could have

we could not

we did not

we do

we do not

we have

we have been

we have been able

we have not

we have not been

we have not been able

we hope

we hope that

we hope that the

we hope the

we hope you are

we hope you will

we hope you will be

we know

we may

we may be

we may be able

we may have

we might

we might be

we might be able

we might have

we need

we think

we will

we will be

we will be able

we will be glad

we will have

we will not

we will not be	with that	you have been able
we will not be able	with the	you have not
we will not have	with you	you have not been
	with your	you have not been able
we would	would be	you may be
we would be	would be able	you may have
we would be able	would be glad	you might
we would be glad	would have	you might be
we would have	would have been	you might be able
we would not	would not	you might have
we would not be	would not be	you might not
we would not be able	would not be able	you order
we would not have	would not have been	you will
well known	you are	you will be
when the	you are not	you will be able
which is	you can	you will be glad
who can	you can be	
will be	you can have	you will have
will be able	you cannot	you will not
will be glad	you could	you will not be
will have	you could be	you will not be able
will not	you could have	you will not have
will not be	you could have been	you would
will not be able	you could not	you would be
will not have	you could not have	you would be able
will you please	you have	you would be glad
with our	you have been	you would have

you would have been

you would not

you would not be

you would not be able

you would not have

your order

Yours cordially

Yours sincerely

Yours truly

Yours very sincerely

Yours very truly

PART 4

NAMES

WOMEN

Abby

Adelaide

Adele

Agnes

Alberta

Alexandria

Alice

Amelia

Amy

Angela

Ann

Anita

Annabelle

Antoinette

Arlene

Barbara

Bertha

Bessie

Beth

Betsy

Betty

Blanche

Bonnie

Camilla

Carmen

Carmelita

Carol

Catherine

Cecilia

Charlotte

Christine

Claire

Clara

Clementine

Constance

Cynthia

Daphne

Deborah

Della

Diana

Dolores

Donna

Doris

Dorothy

Edith

Edna

Eileen

Elaine

Eleanor

Elizabeth

Ellen

Elsa

Emily

Emma

Estelle

Esther

Ethel

Eunice

Eve

Evelyn

Felicita

Florence

Frances

Francesca

Gail

Gertrude

Gloria

Grace

Harriet

Helen

Inez

Irene

Iris

Isabel

Jane

Janice

Jean

Jennifer

Jill

Jo	Madeline	Norma
Joan	Madge	Olga
Joanne	Marcy	Pamela
Jody	Margaret	Pat
Juanita	Margarita	Patricia
Judith	Maria	Patsy
Judy	Marian	Paula
Julie	Marilyn	Pearl
Juliet	Marion	Peggy
Karen	Marjorie	Phyllis
Kathleen	Marsha	Polly
Kathy	Martha	Priscilla
Katie	Mary	Rachel
Laura	Maureen	Ramona
Lillian	Meg	Rebecca
Linda	Melissa	Rita
Lisa	Mercedes	Roberta
Lois	Michelle	Robin
Loretta	Mildred	Rosa
Lorraine	Miranda	Rosalie
Louella	Molly	Rosario
Louise	Monica	Rosita
Lucretia	Muriel	Roxanne
Lucy	Myra	Ruby
Luz	Nancy	Ruth
Lydia	Nannette	Sally
Mabel	Nellie	Sarah

Shirley

Sue

Susan

Sylvia

Terry

Thelma

Theresa

Tina

Toby

Trudy

Valerie

Victoria

Violet

Vivian

Wanda

Wendy

Wilma

Zelda

MEN

Aaron

Abraham

Adam

Albert

Alexander

Alfonso

Alfred

Allen

Andrew

Angelo

Anthony

Antonio

Arnold

Arthur

Barry

Benjamin

Bernard

Bill

Bob

Boris

Boyd

Bradley

Brian

Caesar

Camilo

Carl

Carlos

Charles

Chester

Christopher

Clarence

Claude

Clyde

Craig

Daniel

David

Dennis

Dick

Dominic

Donald

Douglas

Dudley

Duncan

Dwight

Edgar

Edmund

Edward

Edwin

Elliott

Emerson

Emil

Emmanuel

Enrique		Hector		Keith	
Eric		Henry		Kelly	
Ernest		Herbert		Kenneth	
Eugene		Herman		Kevin	
Everett		Hernandez		Larry	
Felix		Horace		Lawrence	
Felipe		Howard		Lee	
Fernando		Hubert		Leo	
Foster		Hugh		Leon	
Francis		Ignacio		Leonard	
Frank		Irving		Leroy	
Franklin		Isaac		Leslie	
Frederick		Jack		Lester	
Gabriel		Jacob		Louis	
Gary		James		Manuel	
Geoffrey		Jay		Marco	
George		Jerome		Marcus	
Gerald		Jerry		Mario	
Gilbert		Jesus		Mark	
Glenn		Jim		Martin	
Gordon		Joe		Matthew	
Graham		John		Melvin	
Gregory		Jonathan		Michael	
Guillermo		Jose		Miguel	
Harold		Joseph		Milton	
Harry		Juan		Mitchell	
Harvey		Julio		Morris	

Murray

Nathan

Nicholas

Nolan

Norman

Oliver

Oscar

Otto

Owen

Patrick

Paul

Pedro

Perry

Peter

Philip

Rafael

Ralph

Randolph

Raymond

Ricardo

Richard

Robert

Robin

Roland

Ronald

Roy

Rudolph

Rufus

Russell

Samuel

Scott

Seth

Sherman

Sherwood

Sidney

Simon

Solomon

Stanley

Stephen

Stuart

Theodore

Thomas

Timothy

Vernon

Victor

Vincent

Virgil

Wallace

Walter

Warren

Wilbur

Wilfred

William

Winston

Woodrow

Zeke

SURNAMES

Abbott

Abrams

Adams

Adkinson

Alberts

Albright

Alexander

Alford

Allen

Allison

Alvarez

Anderson

Andrews

Anthony

Archer

Armstrong

Arnold

Arthur

Ashley

Atkins

Austin

Avery

Ayers

Bacon

Bailey

Baird

Baker

Baldwin

Ball

Ballard

Banks

Barber

Barker

Barlow

Barnes

Barnett

Barr

Barrett

Barron

Barry

Bartlett

Barton

Bass

Bates

Bauer

Baxter

Beach

Bean

Beard

Beasley

Beatty

Beck

Becker

Belcher

Bell

Bender

Benjamin

Bennett

Benson

Bentley

Benton

Berg

Berger

Bernard

Bernstein

Berry

Best

Billings

Bird

Bishop

Black

Blackburn

Blackman

Blackwell

Blair

Blake

Blanchard

Blevins

Bloom	Brock	Calhoun
Bolton	Brooks	Callahan
Bond	Brown	Camero
Bonner	Brownell	Camp
Boone	Browning	Campbell
Booth	Bruce	Cannon
Bowen	Bruno	Cantrell
Bowers	Bryant	Carey
Boyd	Buchanan	Carlson
Boyer	Buck	Carney
Boyle	Buckley	Carpenter
Bradford	Bullock	Carr
Bradley	Burch	Carson
Bradshaw	Burgess	Carter
Brady	Burke	Carver
Branch	Burnett	Case
Brandt	Burns	Casey
Braun	Burris	Cash
Bray	Burt	Castello
Brennan	Burton	Castro
Brenner	Bush	Chamberlain
Brewer	Butler	Chandler
Bridges	Byers	
Briggs	Byrd	Chaney
Bright	Byrne	Chapman
Britt	Cain	Chappell
Britton	Caldwell	Charles

Chase

Cherry

Childers

Childs

Christian

Christiansen

Churchill

Clark

Clay

Clayton

Clemens

Clements

Cline

Cobb

Cochran

Coffey

Cohen

Cole

Coleman

Collier

Collins

Colon

Colton

Combs

Compton

Conklin

Connelly

Connor

Connors

Conrad

Conway

Cook

Cooley

Cooper

Corbett

Cornell

Costa

Costello

Courtney

Cowan

Cox

Craft

Craig

Cramer

Crane

Crawford

Crockett

Crosby

Cross

Crowley

Cruz

Cummings

Cunningham

Curran

Currier

Curry

Curtis

Dailey

Dale

Dalton

Daniels

Daugherty

Davenport

Davids

Davis

Dawson

Day

Dean

Decker

Delaney

Delgado

Dempsey

Dennis

Denton

Diaz

Dick

Dickerson

Dickinson

Dickson

Dillard

Dillon

Dixon	Eaton	Fields
Dodd	Edmonds	Figueroa
Dodson	Edwards	Finch
Doherty	Elder	Fink
Dolan	Elliott	Finley
Domingo	Ellis	Fisher
Donahue	Ellison	Fitzgerald
Donald	Emerson	Fitzpatrick
Donnell	Emery	Flanagan
Donovan	England	Fleming
Dorsey	English	Fletcher
Dougherty	Erickson	Flores
Douglas	Espinosa	Flowers
Downey	Estes	Flynn
Downing	Evans	Forbes
Downs	Everett	Ford
Doyle	Ewing	Foster
Drake	Farley	Fowler
Driscoll	Farmer	Fox
Dudley	Farrell	Francis
Duffy	Farris	Frank
Duncan	Faulkner	Franklin
Dunlop	Feldman	Franks
Dunn	Ferguson	Frazier
Durham	Fernandez	Frederick
Dwyer	Ferrell	Freeman
Dyer	Field	French

Frey

Friedman

Fritz

Frost

Fry

Fullerton

Fulton

Gaines

Gallagher

Galloway

Gamble

Garcia

Gardner

Garner

Garrett

Garrison

Garza

Gay

Gentry

George

Gibbons

Gibbs

Gibson

Gilbert

Giles

Gill

Gillespie

Gilliam

Gilmore

Glass

Gleason

Glenn

Glover

Godfrey

Goff

Goldberg

Golden

Goldman

Goldstein

Gomez

Gonzalez

Good

Goodman

Goodwin

Gordon

Gorman

Gould

Grady

Graham

Grant

Graves

Green

Greenberg

Greer

Gregg

Gregory

Griffin

Griffith

Grimes

Gross

Gustafson

Guthrie

Gutierrez

Guzman

Haas

Hahn

Haines

Hale

Haley

Hall

Hamilton

Hammond

Hampton

Hancock

Hanna

Hanson

Harder

Harding

Hardy

Harmon

Harper

Harrell	Herman	Holt
Harrington	Hernandez	Hood
Harris	Herrera	Hooper
Harrison	Herring	Hoover
Hart	Hess	Hopper
Hartley	Hester	Horne
Hartman	Hewitt	Horton
Harvey	Hickman	Hoskins
Hastings	Hicks	House
Hatfield	Higgins	Houston
Hawkins	Hill	Howard
Hayden	Hilton	Howell
Hayes	Hines	Hubbard
Haynes	Hinkle	Huber
Head	Hinton	Hudson
Heath	Hobbs	Huff
Hebert	Hodge	Huffman
Heller	Hodges	Hughes
Helms	Hoffmann	Hull
Henderson	Hogan	Humphrey
Hendricks	Holcomb	Hunt
Hendrickson	Holden	Hunter
Henning	Holland	Hurley
Henry	Holley	Hurst
Hensen	Holloway	Hutchinson
Hensley	Holman	Hyde
Herbert	Holmes	Ingram

Irwin	Kennedy	Landry
Jackson	Kent	Lane
Jacobs	Kern	Lang
Jacobson	Kerr	Larkin
James	Kessler	Larson
Jarvis	Key	Law
Jefferson	Kidd	Lawrence
Jenkins	King	Lawson
Jennings	Kinney	Leach
Jensen	Kirby	LeBlanc
Jiminez	Kirk	Lee
Johnson	Kirkland	Leonard
Johnston	Kirkpatrick	Lester
Jones	Klein	Levine
Jordan	Knapp	Levy
Joseph	Knight	Lewis
Joyce	Knowles	Lindsey
Justice	Knox	Little
Kaiser	Koch	Livingston
Kaplan	Kramer	Lloyd
Katz	Krause	Locke
Kaufman	Krueger	Logan
Keith	Kuhn	Long
Keller	Lake	Lopez
Kelly	Lamb	Love
Kemp	Lambert	Lowe
Kendall	Lancaster	Lowery

Lund

Lutz

Lynch

Lynn

Lyon

Lyons

Mack

Mackey

Madden

Maddox

Mahoney

Maldonado

Malone

Maloney

Mann

Manning

Marino

Marks

Marsh

Marshall

Martin

Martinez

Mason

Massey

Mathis

Matthews

Maxwell

May

Mayer

Mayfield

Maynard

Mayo

Mays

McBride

McCabe

McCall

McCann

McCarthy

McCauley

McClain

McClure

McCollum

McConnell

McCormack

McCoy

McCullum

McDaniels

McDermott

McDonald

McDowell

McFadden

McFarland

McGee

McGill

McGinnis

McGowan

McGrath

McGuire

McIntosh

McIntyre

McKay

McKee

McKenna

McKenzie

McKinnon

McKnight

McLaughlin

McLean

McLeod

McMahon

McMillan

McNamara

McNeil

McPherson

Meadows

Medina

Melton

Mendez

Mendoza

Mercer

Merrill

Merritt

Metcalf

Meyers

Middleton

Michaels

Milendez

Miles

Miller

Mills

Minor

Mitchell

Molinar

Monroe

Montgomery

Moody

Moon

Mooney

Moore

Morales

Moran

Moreno

Morgan

Morris

Morrison

Morrow

Morse

Morton

Moser

Moses

Mosley

Moss

Moyer

Mueller

Mullen

Munoz

Murphy

Murray

Myer

Myers

Nash

Neal

Nelson

Newell

Newman

Newton

Nichols

Nicholson

Nielsen

Nixon

Noble

Nolan

Norman

Norris

Norton

Novak

O'Brien

O'Connell

O'Connor

Odell

Odom

O'Donnell

Oliver

Olson

O'Neal

Orr

Ortiz

Osborne

Ott

Owen

Owens

Pace

Padilla

Page

Palmer

Park

Parker

Parks

Parrish

Parsons

Pate

Patrick

Patterson

Patton

Paul

Payne

Pearce

Pearson

Peck

Pedersen

Pena

Pennington

Perez

Perkins

Perry

Peters

Petersen

Peterson

Petty

Phillips

Pickett

Pierce

Pierson

Pike

Pittman

Pitts

Pollard

Pool

Pope

Potts

Powell

Powers

Preston

Price

Prichard

Prince

Proctor

Pruitt

Pryor

Pugh

Quinn

Ramirez

Ramos

Ramsey

Randall

Randolph

Rankin

Rasmussen

Ray

Raymond

Reed

Reese

Reeves

Reilly

Reyes

Reynolds

Rhodes

Rice

Rich

Richard

Richards

Richardson

Richmond

Richter

Riddle

Riggs

Riley

Rios

Ritchie

Ritter

Rivera

Rivers

Roach

Robbins

Roberson

Roberts

Robertson

Robinson

Robison

Rodriguez

Rogers

Rollins

Roman	Savage	Short
Romero	Sawyer	Siegel
Rose	Schaefer	Silva
Rosen	Schiller	Silver
Rosenberg	Schmitt	Silverman
Ross	Schneider	Simmons
Rossi	Schoemaker	Simon
Roth	Schreiber	Simpson
Rowe	Schroeder	Sims
Rowland	Schultz	Singer
Roy	Schwartz	Single
Rubin	Scott	Skinner
Ruiz	Sears	Slater
Rush	Sellers	Slaughter
Russell	Sexton	Sloan
Russo	Shaffer	Small
Rutherford	Shannon	Smith
Ryan	Shapiro	Snow
Salazar	Sharpe	Snyder
Sampson	Shaw	Solomon
Sanchez	Shea	Sorensen
Sanders	Sheehan	Soto
Sanford	Shelton	Sparks
Santiago	Shepard	Spears
Santos	Shepherd	Spencer
Sargent	Sherman	Springer
Saunders	Shield	Stafford

Stanley	Talley	Vogel
Stanton	Tate	Wade
Stark	Taylor	Wagner
Starr	Temple	Waldron
Steele	Terrell	Walker
Stein	Terry	Wall
Steinberg	Thompson	Wallace
Steiner	Thornton	Waller
Stern	Todd	Walls
Stevens	Torres	Walsh
Stevenson	Townsend	Walter
Steward	Tracy	Walters
Stewart	Travis	Walton
Stokes	Tucker	Ward
Stone	Turner	Ware
Stout	Tuttle	Warner
Streeter	Tyler	Warren
Strickland	Underwood	Washington
Strong	Valdez	Waters
Stuart	Vance	Watkins
Sullivan	Vandermeer	Watson
Summers	Vargos	Watts
Sutherland	Vasquez	Webb
Sutton	Vaughan	Weber
Swanson	Vega	Webster
Sweeney	Velez	Weeks
Sweet	Vincent	Weiss

Welch

Wells

Welsh

Werner

West

Whalen

Wheeler

Whitaker

White

Whitehead

Whitfield

Whitney

Whitten

Wiggens

Wilcox

Wilder

Wiley

Wilkins

Wilkinson

Williams

Williamson

Willis

Wills

Wilson

Winkler

Winters

Wise

Witt

Wolfe

Wong

Wood

Woodard

Woodruff

Woods

Woodward

Wooten

Workman

Wright

Wyatt

Wynn

Yates

Yong

York

Ziegler

Zimmerman

P A R T

5

GEOGRAPHIC NAMES

STATES

Alabama (AL)
Alaska (AK)
Arizona (AZ)
Arkansas (AR)
California (CA)
Colorado (CO)
Connecticut (CT)
Delaware (DE)
Florida (FL)
Georgia (GA)
Hawaii (HI)
Idaho (ID)
Illinois (IL)
Indiana (IN)
Iowa (IA)
Kansas (KS)
Kentucky (KY)
Louisiana (LA)
Maine (ME)
Maryland (MD)
Massachusetts (MA)
Michigan (MI)
Minnesota (MN)
Mississippi (MS)
Missouri (MO)

Montana (MT)
Nebraska (NE)
Nevada (NV)
New Hampshire (NH)
New Jersey (NJ)
New Mexico (NM)
New York (NY)
North Carolina (NC)
North Dakota (ND)
Ohio (OH)
Oklahoma (OK)
Oregon (OR)
Pennsylvania (PA)
Rhode Island (RI)
South Carolina (SC)
South Dakota (SD)
Tennessee (TN)
Texas (TX)
Utah (UT)
Vermont (VT)
Virginia (VA)
Washington (WA)
West Virginia (WV)
Wisconsin (WI)
Wyoming (WY)

CITIES

Akron
Albany
Albuquerque
Atlanta
Baltimore
Bangor
Birmingham
Bloomington
Boston
Bridgeport
Brownsville
Buffalo
Burlington
Cambridge
Camden
Canton
Centerville
Charleston
Charlotte
Chicago
Cincinnati
Cleveland
Columbus
Dallas
Dayton

Denver

Des Moines

Detroit

Duluth

Elizabeth

Erie

Evansville

Fairfield

Fargo

Fort Worth

Greensburg

Greenville

Harrisburg

Hartford

Honolulu

Huntington

Indianapolis

Jacksonville

Juneau

Kansas City

Knoxville

Lancaster

Lansing

Las Vegas

Lexington

Little Rock

Los Angeles

Louisville

Macon

Madison

Memphis

Mesa

Miami

Midland

Milwaukee

Minneapolis

Mobile

Moline

Montgomery

Montpelier

Nashville

New Bedford

New Orleans

New York

Newark

Newburgh

Oakland

Omaha

Orlando

Peoria

Philadelphia

Phoenix

Pittsburgh

Plainfield

Portland

Providence

Raleigh

Reno

Richmond

Ridgewood

St. Louis

St. Paul

Salt Lake City

San Antonio

San Francisco

Scottsdale

Seattle

Spokane

Springfield

Stamford

Tampa

Trenton

Tucson

Tulsa

Westfield

Westport

Wichita

Wilmington

Woodland

COUNTRIES AND FOREIGN CITIES

Acapulco

Adelaide

Albania

Alberta

Alexandria

Algiers

Amsterdam

Angola

Ankara

Antwerp

Arabia

Argentina

Armenia

Aruba

Athens

Auckland

Australia

Austria

Baghdad

Bahamas

Bangkok

Beirut

Belfast

Belgium

Belgrade

Berlin

Bermuda

Bolivia

Bombay

Bonn

Bordeaux

Brazil

Brisbane

Bristol

Bucharest

Budapest

Buenos Aires

Burma

Cairo

Cambodia

Canada

Canton

Cape Town

Capri

Chile

China

Cologne

Colombia

Costa Rica

Cuba

Cyprus

Czechoslovakia

Dacca

Damascus

Delhi

Denmark

Dover

Dresden

Dublin

Dunkirk

Ecuador

Edinburgh

Edmonton

Egypt

England

Finland

France

Frankfurt

Germany

Ghana

Glasgow

Granada

Great Britain

Greece

Guatemala

Guinea

Haiti

Hamburg

Hanoi

Heidelberg	Lithuania	Oslo
Helsinki	Liverpool	Ottawa
Holland	London	Oxford
Honduras		Pakistan
Hong Kong	Luxembourg	Palestine
Iceland	Lyons	Panama
India	Madagascar	Paraguay
Indonesia	Madrid	Paris
Iran	Majorca	Perth
Iraq	Malta	Peru
Ireland	Manila	Poland
Israel	Marseilles	Portugal
Istanbul	Mexico	Puerto Rico
Italy	Milan	Rio de Janeiro
Jamaica	Montreal	Riviera
Japan	Nanking	Rome
Johannesburg	Naples	Rotterdam
Jordan	Nassau	Rumania
Kenya	Netherlands	Russia
Korea	Newfoundland	Saigon
Laos	Nigeria	Salvador
Latvia	Norway	Salzburg
Lebanon	Nottingham	San José
Leipzig	Nova Scotia	San Juan
Liberia	Nuremberg	Santiago
Libya	Odessa	Sardinia
Lisbon	Ontario	Saudi Arabia

Scotland

Seoul

Serbia

Shanghai

Siberia

Sicily

Singapore

Spain

Suez

Sweden

Switzerland

Sydney

Syria

Tahiti

Tehran

Tel Aviv

Thailand

Tibet

Tokyo

Toronto

Trinidad

Tripoli

Turkey

Ukraine

United States

Uruguay

Valparaiso

Vancouver

Venezuela

Venice

Versailles

Vienna

Vietnam

Wales

Warsaw

West Indies

Yugoslavia

Yukon

Zagreb

Zanzibar

Zurich

365 Great
Barbecue & Grilling
Recipes

Lonnie Gandara
with Peggy Fallon

A JOHN BOSWELL ASSOCIATES BOOK

1817

HARPER & ROW, PUBLISHERS, New York
Grand Rapids, Philadelphia, St. Louis, San Francisco
London, Singapore, Sydney, Tokyo, Toronto

365 GREAT BARBECUE &
GRILLING RECIPES. Copyright ©
1990 by John Boswell Management,
Inc. All rights reserved. Printed in
the United States of America. No
part of this book may be used or
reproduced in any manner
whatsoever without written
permission except in the case of
brief quotations embodied in critical
articles and reviews. For information
address Harper & Row, Publishers,
Inc., 10 East 53rd Street, New York,
N.Y. 10022.

Design: Nigel Rollings
Index: Maro Riofrancos

LIBRARY OF CONGRESS CATALOG CARD NUMBER 89-45655
ISBN 0-06-016295-3

BOMC offers recordings and compact discs, cassettes
and records. For information and catalog write to
BOMR, Camp Hill, PA 17012.